To Tiff,
Do whatever it takes
to find your fortune!

♡
Katie

Fortune
is in the
Failure

Fortune is in the Failure

What you say in business, matters

KATIE MYERS

FORTUNE IS IN THE FAILURE:
What You Say in Business, Matters
Published by CR Conversations
Denver, Colorado
Copyright ©2017 KATIE MYERS. All rights reserved.

Library of Congress Control Number: 9781974137077
MYERS, KATIE, Author
FORTUNE IS IN THE FAILURE:
What You Say in Business, Matters
KATIE MYERS

ISBN: 978-1974137077

BUSINESS & ECONOMICS / Sales & Selling / General
BUSINESS & ECONOMICS / Mentoring & Coaching

QUANTITY PURCHASES: Schools, companies, professional groups, clubs, and other organizations may qualify for special terms when ordering quantities of this title. For information, email Katie@crconversations.com.

This book is printed in the United States of America.

Book Design by Perspektiiv Design Co.

DEDICATION

To my family, Henry, and my mentors:
because of your belief in me,
you helped me find my fortune.

TABLE OF CONTENTS

FOREWORD

–Success rocks. Failure doesn't. Have you ever looked up and wondered when, where, how and if success will ever come? In comes the dreaded failure; that lingering feeling that is always standing in front of you. Do you ever really know how to get around it, break through it and even squash it? As an entrepreneur, failure is one of the biggest fears, probably on the planet. It wasn't talked about. It wasn't thought about. It wasn't dealt with…

…until Katie Myers decided to do something about it!

Katie Myers is brilliant. Her simplistic approach to crushing failure through unique and refreshing steps led me to change the face of my growing company and opened new doors of opportunity simply by changing up language, approach, timing and follow up. My business will never be the same because of Katie and I am forever grateful. Her program is so strong and delivers sustainable results that I now ensure my entire audience is in front of her, so they too can see and experience a new level of success. I get the entrepreneur thing big time. I work with entrepreneurs on how to scale and grow their business and programs to new heights. It is difficult, yet rewarding work and I too have seen many short falls around fear and around failure. Being an entrepreneur takes a lot of grit, drive, determination and the ability to make positive change. There is one thing to build out your dream brand and company, and another thing to actually go grow it. In my over 25 years of professional and business development experience, I have found that most entrepreneurs struggle with actually taking the leap at following up, building relationships and closing the sale. Yes, to truly ask for the business.

So now it's your turn. I challenge you. If you are tired of being a victim and really ready to do this thing, Fortune is in the Failure will be forever game changing for your business. Say hello to success and squash failure…for good.

Kimberly Alexander, Founder of The Results Map and The Grow Grid Programs. Best-selling author of *The Results Map* and *The Results Map for Women in Biz*
Denver, Colorado

one.

INTRODUCTION

Being a successful entrepreneur starts by recognizing the failures you have overcome. There are hundreds of ways failure, the entrepreneurial F word, confronts an entrepreneur. The biggest fears my clients face are around sales. There is a massive stigma against being a salesperson. The title has a negative connotation and very few business owners will admit to being salespeople.

I have spent over ten years as a sales professional and the last four as an entrepreneur. One day, it dawned on me that clients who came through my door followed a pattern. I began asking a series of questions that led to one certainty: their businesses were failing because my clients weren't connected with the sales aspect of their work. Feelings of fear and intimidation, a concern about a lack of experience, and often tears of frustration are common. Despite having an extraordinary passion for the way they served their clients, there was a disconnect from their methods for driving revenue. Why weren't they seeing the results they desired?

In short, they were feeling the sting of failure. So here we are. We are going to talk about the entrepreneurial F-word. We are going to use it to become stronger, more powerful, and to reach the goals you have for your business. There is fortune in failure. There is a pot of gold waiting for you at the end of the sales rainbow.

Finding the fortune doesn't always look easy, though. I too have shed tears, have become so frustrated I wanted to quit, and have hidden behind all sorts of excuses. I had to learn to look failure in the eye and appreciate what it could teach me as an entrepreneur and a salesperson. The stories I will share with you will sound familiar and show you that sales isn't really about having that "special something." This isn't Maybelline: no one is born with it. Sales is a learned skill, and the approach I am going to teach you starts with a basic principle. There are two things human beings want more than anything in this world: to be heard and to know that we matter. Together, this knowledge is what differentiates a thriving relationship from a failing one.

Life as an entrepreneur gives us an assortment of relationships to maintain, juggle, and constantly renew. It's hard enough to be present and accountable in our personal lives. On top of that, throw in the parade of clients, prospects, vendors, partners, and employees, and our work gets complicated quickly. The expectations for creating long-lasting, successful and equally satisfying relationships with each of these people is challenging because despite expectations, no one ever talks about how to keep them from failing.

Nor is it easy. It takes dedication, grit, awareness, and constant self-improvement to maintain the relationships that keep your business thriving.

So how do they go wrong? My journey begins with my college experience. Like many people, I graduated college with a degree that I don't use. It took me a long time to realize that I hadn't wasted four years of my life. I went to college to learn

14

to teach high school history. I had my senior internship and realized that I loved being a teacher, but the venue didn't fit. I wasn't meant to teach kids of any age.

While I was in school, I worked for a restaurant. This was one of several service industry jobs I'd had since entering the workforce; I loved being in the restaurant industry. The speed and the constant interaction with people was a perfect fit for me. I learned how to make as much money as I could by delivering excellent service and making suggestions of things to order. I was learning to sell.

One fateful day, I waited on a couple that owned an insurance agency. They saw something in me and struck up a conversation about needing an office manager. The dream of a 9-to-5 schedule and steady pay intrigued me. I went to work for them within two weeks of that first encounter.

At the time I was hired, the agency's office consisted of the agent, one salesperson, and me. The salesperson didn't stay much longer after I was hired. When she left, the sales role fell into my lap.

My business foundation was laid at that agency. The first lesson I learned was to have no fear. I was given a goal of 100 phone calls per day from cold lists, phone books, and "winback" lists. I quickly began to script calls for myself, figuring out how the hell to sell insurance to someone who already had it. (Insurance is a very unsexy thing to sell.) This turned out to be the perfect ground to begin my life as a saleswoman.

During this time, I grew very close to the agent and his wife. I added a tremendous amount of opportunity and many new skills to my toolkit. One day, they received an opportunity out of state, so they sold their agency. With their guidance and mentorship, I found myself working for another agent in town.

But the challenge was gone, and needless to say I didn't stay long. In my hunt for something new, I sought out a commission sales job selling life insurance—a very bold move. There was a great deal of fear without a guaranteed paycheck. This is one of the first times I was faced with the real uncertainty of sales: I alone was responsible for providing a living for myself. Enter the first time I truly felt the fear of failure.

I loved the job though. I was an independent contractor and I quickly reached a second tier of management, training and advising others on how to make calls, sell in homes, and collect referrals that led to quality business. I didn't allow the fear of failure to cripple me. I put that F-word in its place and used it to fuel my success.

This position required me to be gone at least six days a week, and I would often work all seven. I was away from my boyfriend Henry, my family, and my friends. I was on the road driving from Colorado to Oklahoma, Nebraska and Kansas. I became really unhealthy.

One night I came home to Henry feeling completely defeated. I didn't know what I wanted to do with my life. I really loved the training aspect of what I was doing. I loved the idea of being a teacher and I enjoyed being a contractor. However, I had no time to enjoy life outside of work. It was at this moment that I began to think that my college degree was not a waste—there was something I was meant to teach.

So, I called my mentor, the wife of the first agent I worked for. We had kept in touch and she was always the person I would call to gain insight on matters like these. Our conversation ended in an opportunity to go into business together. I was thrilled! I put in my two weeks' notice and became a partner in the new company within a few weeks.

The concept was brilliant. Our company was essentially an outsourced inbound sales organization. We answered the phone for businesses and sold services on their behalf. I quickly joined a popular networking organization and got my feet wet in the world of business.

After a trial period of about 45 days and lots of discussions with my partner, we came to an agreement on how to organize the business. I could work the business 100 percent of the time while my partner was still employed full-time with another organization.

But it wasn't that easy. Our idea was failing. It just wasn't something our market needed.

We agreed that restructuring was appropriate, so off to the business lawyer I went. We discussed the conversation between my partner and I. We outlined the shape of the partnership moving forward.

When I sent the agreement to my partner, something happened: the biggest fault in communication I had ever experienced. The agreement took my partner by surprise. Things took a very nasty turn.

I had hurt her. In response to what I thought was an agreed-upon solution, she portrayed me as manipulative and intentionally destructive to our partnership. The animosity between us grew rapidly, and ultimately undid our company after only three months. Worse than that, we haven't spoken since. Yet another failure had made its mark on my career.

I was devastated. I didn't understand what had happened and never had the opportunity to clear the air. I had to heal and come to terms with what had happened on my own. I was left to assess the failure and find the silver-lining behind it.

The dissolution of our business took place in April 2013. After all the heartache, disbelief, and unanswered questions, I was faced with the biggest opportunity and choice I'd ever had. My ex-partner had given me a taste of entrepreneurship. I had been out in the field, talking to people, learning about their pain points, and collecting reasons for their failures.

I identified that what they truly needed was for their phones to ring! The failures they were experiencing boiled down to trouble with sales. They didn't know what to say to get the phone to ring, and if it did ring, they lacked the skills of converting a prospect in to a life-long relationship. On May 1st, 2013, CR Conversations was born.

There is a very important lesson from each one of the stories I have shared. This lesson birthed the company I own and set me on the path to change the world and ultimately, to write this book. Each relationship that failed came down to either a lack of appreciation or miscommunication. Every experience, every sales position I was in, and every relationship along the way was dressed in failure. In the end, I learned that every relationship, whether it's professional, friendly, romantic, or familial, is a two-way street that operates by making the other person feel valued, loved, and listened to.

So here we are, between the pages of a book and facing a critical time. We have the power to change the world simply by changing the way we communicate. That's all sales is: communication. Every relationship you need to build in your business relies on communication. The fundamentals of relationship-building do not change, whether we call it personal or business.

As you read this book, I challenge you to extinguish the belief that your business and personal lives are separate. We have one life, and that means that we should maintain the same rules for developing relationships. We shouldn't treat our professional relationships any differently than we treat our personal ones. I challenge you to be open to the idea that if you start treating your business relations like you treat your best friends, everything will change for you.

two.

ACCEPTING YOUR FAILURES

Do you remember the golden rule? The one we were taught in kindergarten? "Treat others like you want to be treated." Well my friend, it's time we get back to that and level-up. We live in a world where connectivity is instant and abundant. We can share our daily status updates in seconds, connect with people across the world, and speak our minds, all from behind the safety of our screens. The basis of all relationships starts with making a connection… but unfortunately, though we are connected, we are not connecting. Our abundant ability to connect opens a multitude of doors for the F-word to make its way into our world. In other words, you must be conscientious in each of your conversations.

Let me paint a picture. Imagine that in one fell swoop, all the technology we have become accustomed to vanishes. No Internet (although you may not think it, I remember when there wasn't an Internet or cell phones), no phones, no computers. All that is left is us. We need to be able to articulate our desires, fears, resolutions, and problems. We need to feel heard, have a sense of purpose, and know that we matter.

I understand it is nearly impossible to imagine a world without the ability to instantly connect with someone. My purpose in describing this is not to begin an anti-technology campaign, but rather to emphasize the necessity of being able to connect human-to-human FIRST, then recognize the unbelievable technology we can use to deliver our intent. It is then that we can overcome failure and truly know what it means to be successful.

So, let's roll up our sleeves, put in the time and set the intention of becoming better communicators. The first step to achieving success is to recognize that we can do better. The next time that you go to send an email, make a phone call, or send a social media message, I encourage you to consciously acknowledge that you are going to make the recipient of your communication feel heard and that they matter. Most importantly, you must demand the same in return. Let me say it again, it starts with YOU. If you don't require other people to treat you like you matter, you can't deliver that for someone else. This is the modern-day golden rule: you matter and need to be heard; treat others the same way.

Let's talk business, shall we? Now that we're leading with empathy, let's talk about what that looks like professionally, and how our current sales conversations and communication with others leads to failure. Many entrepreneurs come to me with the same initial obstacle: they're hustling like crazy, meeting tons of people, going to networking events, happy hours and coffee meetings, but then they become stuck. Dead in their tracks, deer-in-headlights stuck.

Many entrepreneurs don't know what to say after their initial interactions or how to move the relationship forward. If they identify someone who could be a great client, they become paralyzed after the first engagement because they don't want to come across as "salesy". Or entrepreneurs go the opposite way, divulging an absurd amount of information and scaring away potential relationships.

Or they meet someone that they could collaborate with but aren't sure how to get the ball rolling without sounding like "I want to collaborate with you so I can get in front of your clients.". They find themselves with stacks and stacks of business cards that haunt their desks, purses and cars. They fear getting rid of them because of the unknown opportunity, but are hindered because again, they don't know what to say. Sound familiar?

Cue the assumptions. What happens when you assume? It doesn't just make an ass out of you and me, it kills our sales pipelines, ruins customer retention, and can put you out of business. We will talk a lot about assumptions, but the first key to dismantling them is to know they're generally bullshit. Assumptions are little worry bubbles we create in our minds; stories about how others see us and how we think they feel about us. Assuming is a dangerous game, and assumptions lead to the demise of our relationships.

As entrepreneurs, we're responsible for selling. We know our services inside and out; no one can sell what you do like you can. Most entrepreneurs didn't get into business because they are crazy good at selling. They got in to business because of their passion for the solutions they offer to the people they serve. This is where it gets tricky. You are responsible for selling your service, which means: generating the leads, taking the prospect through the sales process, providing the service and then retaining that customer for life. If you aren't naturally gifted in selling, which most people aren't, then you need to obtain the skills and processes to become successful. The first step is to acknowledge that sales starts with a conversation.

But it's not just any conversation. You must know exactly how to lead your prospective client through the steps it takes for them to become your client. As we move forward, we will talk a lot about transparency, being direct, and outlining next steps every time you communicate. It is my mission to make sure that you never lose an opportunity or a client through miscommunication or lack of appreciation. This is how you find the fortune in the failure.

three.

UNDERSTANDING
THE FORTUNE

Being an entrepreneur is hard. We face many different challenges and if you are doing this solo, you are wearing dozens of hats. It is tempting to focus on the work that you started your business to do: the fun stuff, the things that light your fire and got you doing this in the first place. Unfortunately, to get to a place where you solely focus on providing your service, there are processes that need to be put in place. You have to accept that you have screwed up, missed opportunities, and have fallen flat on your face at times. By examining error, you can begin to see the fortune in your failures.

There is a lot of noise surrounding entrepreneurs about what comes first and what tools you need to launch your business or get to the next level. Many flashy programs, sexy strategies and enticing get-rich-quick schemes promise to make it easy. One of the most enticing ideas is that you can outsource your sales. Sure, you can, but don't you dare do so until you have learned from your mistakes and developed real expectations for your sales.

Let's be real, nothing about being an entrepreneur is easy.

This shit is hard. It's challenging work. There is no easy road to becoming successful and reaching the point of doing only the things you want to do.

Business is about people, and people are complicated. To fully serve your audience in the way you intend and dedicate your time to them, you need to have processes in place to develop relationships with people. You need to develop relationships with prospects, collaborative partners, and clients. Each of these relationships is delicate and takes time, just like the relationships in your personal life.

There are four main phases of developing relationships that demand an intentional process. I call these phases Start, Share, Secure, and Sell. Together these phases make up The Core Conversations. Each of these processes is built around the tactics needed to develop quality relationships and take a person from prospect to a long-lasting client. Let's peel back the layers of this complicated sales onion and discover the truth behind your failures.

YOU DON'T KNOW
WHO YOU ARE

The first step in becoming successful in your sales conversations is to understand your audience. To understand your audience, you must first understand yourself. Understanding yourself unlocks the key to identifying who you want to attract. When you understand your values, your likes, and your intentions, it becomes easier to attract the right type of person to your business.

One of the most difficult things for entrepreneurs—myself included—to do is commit to an ideal client. There are billions of people in the world and your first thought may be to say, "I serve anyone who…" or "everybody that…" But my friend, I am going to ask you to commit to one persona and one audience, and I will tell you why.

When you decide on an ideal audience, it makes all aspects of your business simpler. When you remove the ambiguity of words like "anyone, everyone, or anybody," you make it easy to identify exactly who you are looking to serve. It also allows individuals to better identify themselves as people who need your services and opens the door for people to refer you to the appropriate contacts.

But none of this starts with them. The process of deciding who you serve begins with who you think YOU are. Many of us were taught that we have two selves: a professional and a personal. We were taught that business isn't personal; we're meant to keep our personal lives to ourselves and to keep things strictly professional in the business world. Well my friend, I think that's bullshit. We have ONE self. We need to share who we are as individuals within the companies we build. After all, people do business with people, not organizations. Your prospects want to work with someone they can relate to, who understands them and can provide a solution to their problems. It is difficult to do business with someone who hides behind their logo, never revealing who they really are.

As entrepreneurs, we pour every ounce of ourselves into our businesses, day in and day out. It is nearly impossible to prevent overlap in our personal and professional lives. It's time to allow for the overlap, but also to be strategic in how you communicate your personal side.

Defining your ideal audience takes time and dedication. This process is the cornerstone you'll need to build the business of your dreams: to only serve the clients that you enjoy working with. It's your right as an entrepreneur to choose your clients. You don't need to settle on whoever comes through your doors. The process of creating your ideal client begins with assessing the likes, hobbies and interests of that person. The exercise below will take you through a series of questions to consider when defining them. You must be specific. Don't give yourself a wide range of answers. Dream up the perfect person that you would like to serve in your business.

Let's see what your persona could look like using examples from clients I have worked with:

PERSONA #1:

Business industry:
A technology company that creates organizational software

Professional type:
Entrepreneur that has been in business for one to three years

Gender:
Female
Age range: 25 – 35

Likes:
Understands technology
Appreciates technology
Loves animals
Involved in social media, Facebook especially

Dislikes:
Being disorganized, wasting time figuring out software

Hobbies:
Reads professional development books, articles and blogs

Pain points:
Frustrated because she is by herself in her business
Doesn't have enough time to complete all her tasks

What do they offer:
Has products to sell

Where do they shop:
Shops at Nordstrom, Macy's, Target and Whole Foods

Who do they follow/admire: Gary V.

PERSONA #2:

Business industry:
A business coach

Professional type:
Solo entrepreneur

Gender:
Female

Age range:
45 – 55

Education/family status:
College educated Mother

Likes:
To be self-reliant, to be inspired

Hobbies:
Watches the Lifetime channel, the Oprah Winfrey Network and Modern Family
Loves wine
Involved in female networking groups

Pain points:
Has never had sales experience, fearful of being salesy

What do they offer:
One-on-one consulting and workshops

Where do they shop:
Target, Kohl's and King Soopers

Who do they follow/admire:
Follows Marie Forleo and Amy Porterfield

Take some time to fill out the worksheet below to begin to identify your ideal audience.

Business Industry: what industries do you tend to work with?

_____

_____

Professional type: solo-entrepreneurs, employee, executive etc.

_____

Male or female:

_____

Age range within ten years:

_____

Likes and values—what are the things they enjoy? What do they value most in life?

_____

_____

Dislikes—what do they avoid? What are the things they won't put up with?

_____

_____

Where do they shop?

_____

_____

What are their hobbies?

_____

_____

Who do they follow or admire? This could be celebrities, authors, coaches, etc.

_____

_____

What are their current business problems or pain points?

_____

_____

Take a step back and review your answers. Did you answer these questions the way that YOU would personally? Chances are there is a great deal of similarity between you and your ideal client. When we look at who we would like to serve, we are drawn to people who match our own values. You've heard the adage "birds of a feather flock together," right? The same applies here. We all want to work with people who value what we do, share the same outlook, and are enjoyable to work with! People like that tend to stick together and grow together.

When we combine this sweet little recipe of likes, interests, hobbies and values, out comes a fresh-baked ideal client! You've probably discovered that your ideal client...is YOU! You want to attract people you will get along with. There is nothing worse than taking on a client you know in your gut is wrong for you and whom you must constantly battle on how you run your business.

Does that sound familiar? Have you ever taken on a client because you wanted to help them, you needed the revenue, or simply because they wanted to work with you? What happened? The repercussions of taking on a client you don't connect with can be tremendous and leave you needing a way to let that little ship sail off into the ocean.

Now that you've defined your ideal client, it's time to talk about how to communicate in a way that will draw those clients to you. To do that, you need to start sharing—incorporating your personal life into your professional life. For example, I love animals. Dogs especially, but I get all giddy when talking about any animal. When I started to own that animals play a large part in my personal life and shared that element outwardly as part of my brand, the people I found myself attracting were (no surprise) also huge animal lovers!

Now you may be thinking to yourself, what do communication strategies and sales conversations have to do with dogs? There are lots of things we can learn about communication from animals, like curiosity, loyalty, and how to be open to new experiences and interactions. By sharing my support for animal-related causes, pictures of my own fur babies, and participating in community fundraisers for animal shelters, I became a real person to my audience. My business wasn't just business, it was real and relatable and a hell of a conversation starter! Most of my meetings with new clients now start with stories of our animals' antics and how much we love our pets.

My challenge to you is to pick one thing to start with. What is that one hobby or interest that you could share with the world? We've all heard that people do business with people they know, like, and trust, right? Well, how are they going to get to know or like you if all you share about is strictly around the service you offer? Catch my drift? You've got to open up by sharing something about yourself that is relatable to your ideal client. It wasn't until I owned who I was as an individual that I truly understood what type of business I wanted to run.

Let me take you back a few years in my own business. When I first started out, I wasn't represented in my brand. My business cards had an orange-and-blue logo, even though I despise the color orange unless it's on a Denver Broncos jersey. The name of my company, Pure Communication, didn't represent the service I was providing and wasn't attracting my ideal client. The brand was confusing. Because I was hiding behind a brand that wasn't me, people didn't know what I did or who I was.

Shortly before my aha moment, I had participated in a trade show that gave me an opportunity to showcase my business. I ordered embroidered polo t-shirts with my logo on them. I hate polos and, as I mentioned, orange. I had this perception that the colors of my brand, the services I offered, and my engaging personality were all I needed to have a successful company. I was dead wrong.

I realized that if I was disconnected from my brand, it was no wonder others were too. I hated my colors and my outfits. I was attracting clients I didn't enjoy working with. I wasn't living to my full potential, so I did the persona exercise.

This introspective activity empowered me to own WHO I AM. CR Conversations (in plum purple and lime green) was born. I stopped being who I thought everyone else wanted. As soon as I owned my love for purple, for animals, my expertise, and my sassy attitude, I felt at home. Immediately people started to understand who I was and what I did. I began attracting the clients of my dreams. I laugh with them, share stories with them, and provide them with services without ever wondering if they get me.

YOU DON'T OWN THAT YOU'RE A SALESPERSON

If you are struggling to get new clients, it's often because you don't consider yourself a salesperson. This is a common problem that occurs because of a stigma around the word "sales." If you find yourself having trouble accepting that you can be a salesperson, you are creating a limiting belief.

A limiting belief is a belief that is drawn from a false conclusion. They stop us from moving forward—they are the head trash that keeps us from being able to convert prospects into clients or even attracting prospects in the first place. No one likes to be sold to, but that's how business gets done. One person sells the service and the other purchases the service: that's sales. If you are on the side of the table delivering an opportunity for someone to purchase what you are offering, you are selling.

A common fear around sales is that the other person will think you are only trying to sell them something. You must own that you are in fact trying to sell them something; that isn't the real issue. The real issue is the approach you take to what you're selling.

If the work feels salesy, consider re-evaluating what you're saying. You need to be able to get your message across effectively. You must be able to tell others who you are, who you serve, what problems you solve, and what solutions you bring to the table. You must be an effective communicator, which starts by becoming crystal clear on who you want to attract and being able to voice that to them.

This makes first impressions essential. First impressions are all we get. There are no do-overs. People make up their minds about us quickly, so we need to deliver the best first impression possible.

I like to refer to your first impression as your introductory message. There are several scenarios where you'd deliver your introductory message and attract interest. Traditionally, you will have the opportunity to give a commercial or elevator pitch at networking events. You may have the chance to formally present your commercial to an entire group, or it could be in a more casual setting at a happy hour event or conference. The first key is to keep your message consistent no matter what environment you're in.

The best way to diagnose if the reason you are failing in your sales conversations has to do with your messaging is to look for these signs:

- **They just aren't that into you.** During your opportunity to share, your audience shows signs of disinterest: fake smiles, no emotion, no eye contact, not taking notes, or becoming distracted by their phones.

- **There aren't any follow-up questions.** This is a tricky one. People often think that if an audience doesn't ask questions, it means they fully understood what you said. In reality, it is usually the opposite. You want to lead them to ask more open-ended questions, including "Tell me more about how you do that," "How did you come up with that?" "That sounds interesting," and "I'd love to learn more."

- **There is no second date.** The intent of networking is to meet someone, then take them to the next step in the relationship. If you aren't getting people who ask to schedule a time to chat, give you their business card or ask for yours, or try to continue the conversation in any form, it's not them, it's you.

I want to be clear: not *everyone* is going to be your ideal audience. So be wary of getting defeated by the above scenarios if you aren't talking to the right audience. If you are clear on who you are, who you serve, and how you serve, you will quickly be able to identify the right people to work with.

The key to creating long-lasting relationships begins by setting the groundwork through that first impression. The moment that you meet or interact with a prospective client, collaborative partner, vendor, or affiliate partner is the moment you determine how you are going to be treated and how you will treat them. Making them feel heard and that they matter begins immediately. One of the simplest ways to convey this is to ask them about their preferred method of communication. It's awfully simple, but can make a significant impact. Why?

When you ask someone how they'd like to be contacted it does two things. First, it acknowledges their needs (the "matter" part), and it gives you instructions for how to approach them (the "heard" part). Right out of the gate, you've laid the first brick of appreciation and good communication. The second thing this does is empower you to anticipate when someone is likely to engage with you. You've already learned the easiest way to get ahold of that person as you continue to build your relationship.

Another very important fact is that fully-developed professional relationships require multiple forms of communication. You won't just be using their preferred form of contact—it's important not to sacrifice your own comfort and abandon your preferences. You need to voice your preferences to assure that reciprocity is possible. I recognize that not everyone communicates best in the same way, especially with the number of options available to connect.

I once worked with a woman who wanted to book me for a speaking engagement. She contacted me on Facebook Messenger, my least-preferred form of communication for work. I'm a phone call person. When I realized that she had been trying to get ahold of me, I let her know that I preferred discussing these matters on the phone, but if Facebook messenger was better for her, we could perhaps find some middle ground. We ended up settling on text messaging. Needless to say, it was much easier for us to finalize our agreement and for her to book me as a speaker.

Setting yourself up for success begins with the very first encounter, whether it's an email introduction, a meeting at a networking event, or a meeting with an audience you have spoken or presented to. If you lead with the intention of relationships founded on appreciation and crystal-clear communication, you will build relationships faster, which leads to gaining revenue faster and a break from being in constant hustle mode.

Many people fail right out of the gate. They attend a networking event or opportunity to meet other entrepreneurs and only talk about one thing: themselves. They word-vomit all the things they do without considering that they are participating in a conversation, not a monologue. People want to make connections now more than ever. People want to be involved in conversations, to feel heard, and to know they matter. Once you understand that initial principle and connect it with the mission and vision of your business, you will be able to build relationships with your audience. How many times have you heard someone at a networking event say, "I'm not a pushy salesperson, I am about building relationships?" Probably quite a few times, right? You may have even said that about yourself. But there are ways of selling that are positive and attractive to others. Being a confident salesperson and an entrepreneur is a positive trait.

Be wary that some entrepreneurs who say they are about building relationships, actually view their clients as numbers. That is the difference between a salesperson who wants longevity and one who is looking for a quick fix. You are here to build a business, not a fly-by-night operation. Relationship building is the key to successful sales conversations. You must recognize that if you are serious about making long-lasting connections, you need to be strategic and generate sustainable ones. If you say you're about building relationships, you'd better mean it. If you don't have a strategy, then you have a problem. The good news is, you can become genuine in your delivery with the right perspective. That should feel a lot less salesy.

YOUR MESSAGE IS UNCLEAR

Clear messaging is tricky. Part of getting it right involves getting over ourselves and speaking in our prospect's language, not just from our own expertise. We face our insecurities when first stepping out in to the world to tell others what we do. The natural response is to share the wealth of information you have in your line of work. Though it may feel necessary to puff up your chest and show how much you know, it's a huge turn-off and can be confusing to your ideal client.

You can feel exposed and find a lot of head trash that gets in the way of your true message when you get up in front of a networking group to share or introduce yourself at an event. The trick to overcoming these insecurities is to own who you are as a person first, then as a company or brand. You can then deliver your message with confidence, not boastfulness.

If there is anything I have learned about building genuine personal and professional relationships, it's that we must look inward to move upward. Again, it all starts with YOU. You must set the intention of clearly communicating what type of business you run and who you serve in that business in a way your audience can understand. This requires rolling up your sleeves and doing the work required to build the foundation.

If you don't have a strategy and intention for your messaging, there is no point in sharing it. In all likelihood, you'll wind up rambling and never make a connection with anyone. You don't want to create that impression. Your business is helpful to others, right? Then you are impacting the lives of those you serve. Take this into consideration when you are working on your messaging.

You may not see your service offering or product as something that directly changes someone's life, but it does. Here is an example: I have a client who is a health coach. She uses products from a well-known health and wellness company as a tool to help her clients embrace a healthy lifestyle. I encouraged her to think about her ideal client. She serves women between the ages of 35 and 45 who are experiencing a new decade in life and new changes in their bodies. She changes the lives of her clients by giving them the tools to return to physical activities they engaged in when they were younger. Their lives change because they feel more confident, which in turn helps them be more present in their other relationships. They have more energy to play with their kids, which makes them better parents. By connecting her message with real scenarios her clients were experiencing, her ideal prospects could identify themselves.

Working through your messaging is an evolutionary process. It will change, it will morph, and it will be something that you re-evaluate throughout your career. Below are some exercises to get you started in producing your introductory message.

Definition of messaging: It is imperative that your messaging speaks directly to who you are serving. From your tagline to the content on your website, it needs to remain consistent and concise.

What services do you offer? List all the ways you can help your ideal client, such as one-on-one consulting, workshops, DIY options, or products.

_____

_____

_____

_____

What is the main objective of someone hiring you? What is the problem they are having?

_____

_____

_____

What are keywords that describe what you do? Use this space to brainstorm. How would someone else describe your service to others?

_____

_____

_____

How do you want your clients to feel when and after working with you? What you do is impactful. Find words that showcase the outcome your clients have after working with you.

_____

_____

_____

_____

_____

How do you change the lives of your clients? What impact are you making in their lives when providing solutions to their problems?

_____

_____

_____

Take the space below to think about how you serve and how it changes the lives of your clients:

_____

_____

_____

_____

_____

_____

_____

_____

Now that you've uncovered the foundation of your messaging, it's time to define your core message. Your core message is your elevator pitch, a 30-second go-to description of who you are, how you serve, and who you serve. It is essential to have this message locked and loaded, ready to communicate to anyone you meet. The next exercise explores how to appropriately position your core message so that it is clear, concise, and easy for others to comprehend.

Defining your Core Message

Define your core message: Your core message should be about 30 seconds long when recited aloud, and contain three main components:

- Who you are—your name and company

- How you serve—the problem your clients have and how you deliver your service

- How you solve—the solution you provide to overcome the problem of your ideal client

_____

_____

_____

_____

_____

_____

_____

_____

_____

_____

Dialing in on your core messaging takes repetition and practice. Some of the things to consider and apply in your practice include:

- **Confide in those you trust.** Share your introductory message with someone who will give you honest feedback. After you recite your core message, ask that person to repeat back the explanation of what you do. This exercise can be very telling. When someone tells you what they think you do, it can shed light on the confusion you may be putting out in the world. The key to this is to share with people you can trust to give you honest and constructive feedback. This might be a business coach, people in your networking group, or a mentor.

- **Hire a coach or strategist.** We all have our talents. Recognize that if creating clear messaging or having a strategy for bringing in clients is not your strong suit, you need to ask for help. The advice I use when hiring my own help is to find someone with a proven track record who has done it themselves!

- **Work with someone with a specialty.** When hiring a coach or strategist to help you, look for a messaging specialist. I caution you to avoid a jack-or-jane-of-all-trades coach for this problem.

- **Practice makes perfect.** While you are driving in your car, watching TV, cooking dinner, or whenever you have time, recite your messaging out loud. This exercise will strengthen the messaging muscles you need to sound confident—an attractive quality to someone looking for your service.

The process of reconnecting with your message or creating messaging for the first time can be challenging. Give yourself some grace. Finding your genuine place is one of the hardest pieces of being an entrepreneur. So, stay true to who you are and share with your audience your personality, likes, and interests. People want connection and you want to attract the people who will instantly get what you do and identity themselves as the right client for you. Be real. Be clear. Be confident. That's the recipe for a strong foundation.

seven.

YOU USE SPAGHETTI VS. STRATEGY

One day, a client sat down in my office for her first strategy session with me. She looked flustered and frustrated. She took a deep breath and said, "I'm tired of flying by the seat of my pants and hoping I will get the business I need." I reassured her that this was a common feeling for many entrepreneurs and said that structure was all she needed to create sustainability.

Like many entrepreneurs, she had seen some success, gotten a few clients and had a few irons in the fire prospect-wise. But she felt like she was throwing spaghetti at the wall to see what stuck and was tired of waiting to see what would happen in her business.

Sometimes easy-to-get clients will come through your doors. They identify themselves as needing you; perhaps they were referred to you. They are quick to sign the contract and get started. This does happen. The point of having a strategy is to make this happen on a re-occurring basis and to learn what it took for that client to walk through your door so you can repeat the experience.

Part of your structure needs to include proactive communication. Your strategy for meeting new prospects, wooing them to become clients, and keeping them can't wait on someone else. It is easy when we have some success to just go with the flow and see what happens. We get stuck in the "I got the clients this way once, so why not again?" mentality and that's a dangerous, unstable place to be.

Your ideal clients are waiting for you; they have the problem you solve. It takes forethought to know where they are, how they want to be communicated with, and how to present your offerings to them. The first step is to assess what goals you have around your sales. We aren't just talking about a revenue goal. If you aren't money motivated, then putting your efforts towards a revenue goal isn't going to be fruitful. As an alternative, think about the number of people you want to serve, how many people do you want to help? Start with one year.

How many people do you want to serve per year?

Now I want you to think about the last ideal client that came through your doors. Where did they come from? How many people did you meet with to find this qualified prospect? A qualified prospect should fit the characteristics of an ideal client.

How many conversations do you need to have to get one qualified prospect? Think about the last client you landed. Where and when did you meet them? How many people did you meet within that timeframe to get that 1 client? If you aren't sure, take a guess for now.

_____

_____

_____

_____

You must now determine your conversion rates to success-fully have a plan for your sales goals. If you are unsure of the numbers currently, that is okay. Ballpark the numbers. Some quick math will help you determine how many conversations it takes to get 1 qualified prospect. Once you have that figured out then you can decide how many qualified prospects it takes to get 1 client. See the equations below:

$$\frac{\text{Prospects}}{\text{Qualified \# of Conversations}} \boxed{= \text{Qualified Prospect Conversations}}$$

Example: 5 conversations with my ideal audience will get me 1 qualified prospect.

$$\frac{1 \text{ Prospect}}{5 \text{ Conversations}} \boxed{= .20 \text{ or } 20\% \text{ Conversion}}$$

What is your conversion rate for conversations to qualified prospects?

_____

_____

_____

Now, let's determine your client conversion rate.

$$\frac{\text{New Clients}}{\text{Qualified Prospects}} \boxed{= \text{Client Conversion \%}}$$

Example: I know that it takes 2 qualified prospects to get 1 client.

$$\frac{1 \text{ Client}}{2 \text{ Qualified Prospects}} \boxed{= .50 \text{ or } 50\% \text{ Conversion}}$$

Now to figure out how many conversations we need to have to get to the goal of 20 clients for example, we need to work backwards.

For example: If we want 20 clients and we know our conversion rate is 50%..

$$\frac{20 \text{ clients}}{.5} = 40 \text{ qualified prospects}$$

We use this equation one more time to determine how many conversations we need to have with our ideal audience to get 20 clients with this conversion rate being 20%.

$$\frac{40 \text{ qualified prospects}}{.20} = 200 \text{ conversations}$$

How many conversations do you need to have to get the number of clients you want to work with?

_____

_____

_____

You now have real sales goals to work towards. The purpose of this process is for you to know exactly how to spend your time and more importantly, with whom.

Once you've set some goals, it's time to find your ideal audience. How? The best approach is to network. Networking is a beautiful thing; it's an opportunity to meet face-to-face with the people who need your business. When you network, you can meet all categories of potential allies: prospects, collaborative partners, vendors, affiliates, and the lovely "randoms." Networking can be the best funnel-filler for your communication strategy if it is done appropriately.

Networking can be challenging. It starts by figuring out where you should network. The best advice I can give on this is that you just need to start. Use tools like MeetUp.com to search for professional groups around your area. You will need to try different events and organizations on before you nail down what works best for you.

In the first year of my business I went to what seemed like every networking event I could find. I did breakfast meetings, lunch meetings, endless happy hours, mixers, structured meetings, presentations, and workshops. Many I only attended once because the vibe wasn't right or because they just weren't my people. Other times, it was because the people weren't my ideal audience or they didn't hold my core values.

Listen to your gut and find a group that is accepting, support-
ive, and able to elevate you professionally and personally.

Once you find a group you jive with that makes you feel excited to attend, you need to go all-in, no holds barred. You need
to take advantage of everything the organization offers. Below
are ways to fully take advantage of an organization:

- If there are local meetings, go to them consistently and
  put them on your calendar—no wavering.

- If there are Facebook groups or other social media features, get connected.

- Make it a point to fill your calendar with three to four connections with members of that group each week

- Assume a leadership position, if possible. Any time you
  can be in the forefront of an organization offers leverage.
  It makes you and your business more visible.

As an entrepreneur, I've learned many lessons, encountered
many obstacles and seen many successes. I too, have had my
fair share of F-words. All of them have helped me become a
better salesperson and communication strategist. Some of the
most impactful experiences in finding my fortune have been
through networking. Networking has been a great teacher.

To become really good at networking, I had to own who I am. As
I said before, I'm a huge dog-lover. I find an immense amount
of joy when it comes to seeing animals being their naturally
adorable, uninhibited selves. I started observing the behavior of
dogs when I dug my heels in to being an entrepreneur. The first
time I noticed I was making a correlation between how dogs
and humans interact was after a networking event I attended.
We've all been to a happy hour networking event, right? Well

this particular event went like this: when I first walked in, there were crowds and obvious cliques. There was a table of greeters that signed me in, gave me a name badge, then looked right past me to the next person. I was sent off into the pool of people.

First stop, the bar (I sometimes need a little liquid courage to start the conversation sometimes, you feel me?). Scanning the room, I studied the people who were there and started to consider who I was going to chat with first. I saw a group of people standing around as one person dominated the conversation. To my left, there was a group of three women who seemed as if they had known each other for a long time. They were standing very close to one another and occasionally grabbing the outside of each other's arms or patting one another on the back. To my right were two people, one man and one woman. They were clutching their drinks, making awkward eye contact, and engaging in what looked like excruciating small talk.

I received my drink from the bartender (this particular event called for an old-fashioned) and decided to join the latter of the two awkward turtles. I walked up with my hand out to introduce myself and began to ask my usual getting-to-know-you-questions:

"What brings you here tonight?"

"Tell me a bit about yourself!"

"How should I introduce you to others?"

"Who makes up the best collaborative partners for you?"

With those leading questions, both parties began to perk up and engage in the conversation. I positioned my body so it was slightly outward-facing, so others walking by felt like they could pop in to the conversation. Soon other people began coming up to us, introducing themselves, and running through the same questions. The connection process had begun!

So, what does this have to do with dogs? Well, not long after I attended this event, I took my shar-pei, Daphne, to the dog park. I must explain that Daphne was a rambunctious and very vocal pup. She became beside herself when we got to the top of the path where she could see the entrance to the dog park. It was really embarrassing: she squawked like a bird at the sight of her potential playmates.

We entered the dog park and a very familiar feeling came over me. We were instantly greeted at the entrance by four dogs, nose-to-nose with Daphne. They were barking and wagging uncontrollably and seemed as if they could barely stand the anticipation of us walking through the gate. As soon as we entered, another dog mom and her dog came into the park behind us. The "greeting" dogs went right past Daphne and were there to give the same excited welcome to the next pooch, just like the greeters at the networking event.

Once I entered the dog park behind Daphne, I started to observe the dogs in the park. There were all sorts of breeds, sizes and shapes. There were tiny dogs, young dogs, old dogs and everything in between.

What I noticed started to seem awfully familiar once again. As I observed, I noticed there were different social groups of dogs. There were very active dogs constantly chasing one another up and down the dog park. To my right were shy pups that didn't want to leave their parents' side. To my left there were cautious-looking dogs sniffing each other inquisitively and taking their time to decide whether they were going to play or not. And naturally, there were the frisky pups that had one intention and one intention only: yep, lovemaking at the dog park.

I began to internalize what I was seeing, recognizing the similar ways humans and dogs interact. Daphne had to choose what type of group she was going to join. Was she in the mood to run and chase and play? Or was she happy to just sit and observe in the comfort of my shadow?

Key components identified themselves as truths no matter which world I was in, the networking world or the dog park world. In each scenario, the participants had different social groups they had to choose to identify with. They had to muster up courage to enter the establishment and make connections. By observing interactions, I started to sense that we have more to learn from the animal kingdom than we may ever be able to accept. Dogs are miraculous creatures. They are resilient, brave, courageous and undoubtedly loyal. I like to think of myself as one of those dogs entering the dog park when I walk in to a networking event. Which dog do I choose to be? So, I challenge you to consider whether you are a greeter, you encourage others to join you, or you prefer to stand in the shadows and wait to be approached.

Think about your networking principles, your networking values. Take some time to answer the questions below to get a good idea of where you can find your tribe!

What kind of person do you want to be at a networking event? The greeter, the by-stander, the engager etc.

_____
_____
_____
_____
_____

What are your core values?

_____

_____

_____

_____

_____

What type of people are you looking to meet? Think about your ideal client and the persona you built.

_____

_____

_____

_____

_____

What environment do you feel the most comfortable in? (Happy hour, big group, structured meetings, educational events, and so on)

_____

_____

_____

_____

_____

After considering the questions above, you can begin narrowing down your search for places to network. Defining the type of environment where you are comfortable is your right as an entrepreneur. It's up to you to then make the most out of your engagements!

eight.

YOU'RE OUT OF BALANCE

One of the toughest juggling acts we do as entrepreneurs is to make money while also building out our business for growth. There needs to be an equal balance between here-and-now moneymaking and working to develop processes that allow for growth and expansion in the future.

This balancing act is challenging, and missteps can make creating a sustainable business impossible. Most of the entrepreneurs I work with struggle with this. It is an equal focus on building a sales process and follow-up strategy to make the cash register ring right now and developing strategies to keep those customers and continue to serve them in the future.

The solution begins with understanding how to manage your time. One of the best resources I have found on this is The Results Map by Kimberly Alexander. Kimberly recommends negotiating between our personal and professional times, setting strict lines between when we have to be "on" and "off." Time is truly the most important commodity we possess. It's important to manage it carefully.

In The Results Map, you will find an exercise where you make a chart of all your activities and how you spend your time each day, both personally and professionally. It is extremely eye-opening. Because guess what? There are 168 hours in a week. That's it, we can't make more hours. Ironically, we try to. We try to squeeze in 200+ hours of work and home life, which is impossible! I recommend doing the exercise for yourself. You can find it here: kimberlyalexanderinc.com/results-map/the-results-map-worksheets/

Once you have done the exercise and realized that you are just like the rest of us—trying to do more than is possible—you will begin your journey of finding balance.

Something about being an entrepreneur automatically makes us givers. Being a giver means that we are susceptible to not having time for ourselves. We got into business for ourselves to help others with our unique talents. It's the "helping others" part that gets a little tricky. Many of my clients are givers. Their hearts bleed for the problems of others and they want to help any way they can. On the surface, this is an incredible quality. But below the surface, it causes a problem.

If you are constantly giving, there is no room for receiving. If you are constantly giving to people without asking for what YOU need, you're looking at a real problem. To be a successful entrepreneur and serve the people that need you, you must ask for what you need.

Let's take networking, for example. If you are at a networking event, there is a high likelihood that you'll be the one asking questions, trying to see how you can help. Who can you connect them with? How can you make their problems go away? In that conversation, do you ever stop and ask for what you need? Do you make a point to thank them for sharing, and to ask if you can share your needs?

If you're a giver first, the answer is most likely "no." You're just hoping that someone will ask you these questions. You may also assume that because they didn't ask, they aren't interested. Well, my friend, it's time to start asking for what you need. I once had a client who so desperately wanted to help others that she would put her own business on the back-burner unless the subject came up. We worked through the scenarios where she could take control and ask for what she needed in a way that was comfortable for her. As an object lesson, we focused on a getting-to-know you meeting she'd had.

The person she was meeting with was shy. They were uncomfortable and didn't have much experience in the business world, the person my client was meeting with didn't know what to be asking. My client led the conversation for almost an hour, asking tons of questions and seeing how she could help. The hour came and went. At no time was she asked about herself. When we talked about this conversation, I asked her to try using different language. I told her to pay attention to the time, and that when it reached the midway mark— say 30 minutes into the hour they'd scheduled together—to stop and thank the other person for sharing their story. Then, she would ask the other person if it would be all right if she shared hers. A request positioned in a non-threatening, non-salesy way opened the door for her to share about herself.

If you find yourself constantly giving and never asking for what you need, I want you to go back and remind yourself how many people you need to have conversations with. If you're going to get through that, these conversations need to be two-sided, meaning you must ask for what you need. This comes down to rehearsing and having a game-plan for your ask. You need to protect your conversations and make sure you have the opportunity to share about yourself and what you are looking for in your business.

The following are things you should share in each conversation:

Your story: Ask the person you are meeting with if you can share your story. It may feel abrupt, but remember, they are here to learn about you too. Your version should incorporate your background, some personal qualities, and what led you into doing the work you do now.

Practice your story here:

_____
_____
_____
_____
_____
_____
_____
_____

Your ideal client: Share with them who you serve. What type of people are you wanting to work with? How old are they? What are their likes/dislikes? Reflect back on the ideal client persona exercise. Be specific!

_____
_____
_____
_____
_____
_____
_____
_____

Your ask: Ask for what you need! Are you looking to fill a workshop? Do you want to work one-on-one with clients? You always want to know exactly what you are looking for in order to get what you need! Your ask will change, so prepare your ask for 90 days at a time so you can stay consistent.

What are you looking for in the next 90 days?

_____

_____

_____

_____

_____

_____

Whether you are in a networking conversation or meeting someone for a cup of coffee, you need to reserve space and time to ask for what you need. That person may not be your ideal client, but that doesn't mean that they can't connect you with someone who is.

Now you may be thinking, "That sounds selfish and I'm uncomfortable asking for what I need." Get rid of that thought. That's just another limiting belief that can kill your business. You deserve to ask for what you need, just like everyone else does. But it's on you to make space for it. You can't help the people that need you if you aren't telling people how you can help. Got it?

Good. Start asking for what you need.

nine.

YOU'RE UNORGANIZED

One of the most common problems I hear is that my clients have tons of business cards sitting on their desks from people they met at networking events and are paralyzed because they don't know what to say to continue the conversation. So, the stack grows. Perhaps it moves to a cabinet or a nice binder while all the potential of those relationships goes to waste. Those stacks of business cards are gold mines once the right strategy is in place.

In order to tap into that motherlode, you must get organized. There is always heavy lifting upfront—it takes time to get yourself organized to begin sales conversations. You have to roll up your sleeves and dedicate that time to be effective.

The first step in getting organized is to sort your business cards into categories. The intention is to separate your business cards and contacts you've acquired to then add them to a software program called a Customer Relationship Management (CRM) system. I will share more about what to look for in a CRM in chapter ten.

Additionally, organized records make for easy communication. With the right database, you can easily tap into your records anytime from anywhere with an Internet connection. You will no longer be tied to your filing cabinet, or miss out on opportunities because your business cards are in a binder or on your desk. You won't be able to hold on to these things as excuses to avoid sales conversations.

Let's begin the process of categorization. Separate your contacts into five categories:

1. **Prospects:** People you identify as qualified potential clients.

2. **Collaborative Partners:** People who have a complimentary service to yours and share the same target audience. You must have a deep connection and trust with these individuals. See chapter thirteen.

3. **Affiliates:** People who don't have a complimentary service but whom you'd refer if you had the opportunity.

4. **Vendors:** People whose services you are currently using or would potentially use to help your own business. People you would hire.

5. **Randoms:** People you can't recall much about. They don't fit into any of the above categories, or you truly do not remember meeting them. Do not throw these away! There is potential for reconnecting with these individuals. This is the only time you get a do-over at a first impression.

When you are physically sorting these business cards, I want you to put them in piles and bundle them together with a sticky note.

Now let's talk about sorting your existing database, your email contacts or any other digital log of connections. You'll want to use Microsoft Excel or Google Sheets to create a spreadsheet for all five of these categories. You will then want to export your contacts from wherever they are sourced into an Excel spreadsheet. This way you can then copy and paste them from the original lists into the individual spreadsheets for each applicable category.

One last tip when you are constructing your lists: make notes on the cards and within the lists along the way. Give yourself a clue as to who the person is, why they are in that category, and something that you remember about them. Perhaps where you met them originally? This is going to come in extremely handy when you're ready to connect again.

Now I know what you're thinking: "This is going to take forever," or "This is a mundane project." You are right, but only to an extent. It will take time and it won't be the most exciting part of your day. Remember, the longer you wait, the more time it will take to sort. But this work is imperative for setting yourself up to have a successful communication strategy. Once you have your contacts in to the appropriate categories, it's time to go deeper. This part of the process is what I call creating The List: putting all your sorted contacts in to one place. The List is the lifeblood of your company. It's the key to your success and will be central to the growth of your business.

It's now time to revisit The List as a whole and put some real thought into the people you have collected. There are several things that will come up when you're looking at your list. The first is the chatter in your mind that says things like, "This list isn't very big," "These people won't remember me," or the biggest limiter of all, "These people won't want to hear from me."

Creating your list and preparing it so you can start conversations with the people on it can be a difficult process. Know that you are not alone and that all of the head trash you will hear is simply not true. If you follow the processes and build your communication strategy, you will be confident in connecting with the people on your list. Remember: these are just conversations.

Let's address each statement from the previous examples of mind-chatter and identify the truth around it. When you hear the voices telling you "This list isn't very big," I want you to remember this: all it takes is one person. One conversation can change everything. Your list begins with the very first person that is added to it, no matter what category they fall into. You have to start at the beginning, and if you only have one person in your list, then you will focus on that one person and build a relationship with them. When you build a relationship with someone, they will open up their circle of people and make the introductions you need. This is how you populate your list with genuine connections.

"These people won't remember me." If this statement comes up while creating your list, I want you to think about this: the people who don't remember you are now new opportunities to introduce yourself again. You get a do-over! You get a second chance at a first impression. This is really the only time this ever happens. Besides, your business has evolved since the last time you spoke, or maybe you have evolved since the last time you spoke. Seize the opportunity to start fresh.

"These people won't want to hear from me." You may be hearing this because you feel insecure about what you have to say. Worse, you may feel like you have nothing to say at all. Or maybe you don't want to bother people or feel like added noise. All of these feelings are perfectly natural. We never want to feel bothersome.

When you find yourself identifying with these feelings, I want you think about this: you have something special. That something special is you. You have a service to offer that is life-changing and makes an impact. You are doing a disservice to the people that need you if you don't open the door for conversation. And most importantly, if there are people who say, "No thank you" or don't engage with you when you start your strategy, that just makes room for more of the right kind of people.

What negative feelings do you have around contacting the names on your list?

_____

_____

_____

_____

_____

_____

Now replace them with a true, positive statement here:

_____

_____

_____

_____

_____

_____

Repeat this process any time you engage in negative self-talk. Read your positive statements aloud as many times as you can to help re-enforce its truth. Carry a notebook if you need to.

ten.

YOU DON'T HAVE A CRM SYSTEM

Your strategy can't work if you don't have tools in place to get it done. Let's be real for a moment: for many people, sales and follow-up is not the fun part of being an entrepreneur. It's work, it's not sexy, and it takes you doing the work first before you can hand it off to someone else. So, knowing that the success of your business is solely your responsibility, let's talk about the tools you need in order to make it as easy as possible for you to avoid the F-word and be successful. A CRM (Customer Relationship Manager) system will help.

I mentioned the necessity of having a CRM system. When looking, you need to think about the following:

- You need to be able to add your contacts via an Excel file AND individually in the future

- You need to have the ability to easily add notes and review notes in contact accounts

- You want the option to customize fields for your contacts (keep track of their birthdays, contract renewal dates, their dog's names—yes, that's one of my custom fields) etc.

- You will need to have multiple tags so you can easily look at a category of people at a glance

- You need an accountability feature (a pop-up or notification to remind you to take action on a contact)

- You will need an email feature to be able to send mass emails AND individual emails

The most important factor in choosing a CRM is that it has to be easy and user-friendly. For example, I have a 30-minute rule when it comes to technology. If I can't figure out what I need it to do in 30 minutes or less, I move on. I have learned to use this rule in many things in my life and it has allowed me to adopt the systems that are the best fit for my company, my learning styles, and my sanity.

The CRM I recommend is developed by a company started in Colorado, my home sweet home. AllProWebTools (allprowebtools.com) has become my preferred CRM and is the one I recommend to all of my clients.

The second tool you need to incorporate is a scheduling system. A scheduling system is an online program that connects with whatever you use for your email—Outlook, Gmail, iMail, and so on—that allows people to book time with you through a link or a website.

This tool simplifies things immensely. It eliminates the back and forth of trying to schedule a meeting, a consultation with a prospect, and any other gatherings you have in your business. When considering a scheduling system, you will want to think about the following features:

- You need it to connect to your email server

- You need options to create as many appointment types as possible

- You need it to allow you to brand your company on the scheduling page (your logo, your company colors, and so on)

- You need it to allow you to set specific times for each appointment (this is where the balance for your time comes in to play)

As with CRMs, there are dozens of scheduling systems to choose from. I've found Acuity Scheduling, (acuityscheduling. com) to be a great option. Just remember, if you can't figure it out in 30 minutes, bag it and move on to a solution that fits you!

eleven.

YOU JUMP THE GUN

I'll venture to guess that you didn't start your business because you are one hell of a salesperson and decided to sell something of your own. Though there are a few people like that, I am sure that your reason for becoming an entrepreneur is because you are crazy passionate about what you do! You became an entrepreneur to help people, to change lives, to make businesses run easier, and to influence change. So why are we so quick to overlook the fact that we need to be able to successfully share what we offer with our ideal clients?

It's time for a mindset shift. It's time to start thinking about building relationships, not just having transactions. It's time to become a better communicator to understand the phases that your business will go through in attracting prospects and converting them in to lifelong clients. I want you to build relationships that lead to revenue.

Strategy is the vehicle that drives you to your goal. The goal for any successful business is to build lifelong relationships that generate revenue and fuel expansion. My goal when working with clients is to build communication strategies that help them feel comfortable in their own skin and to share their services without any qualms around selling. It's about building relationships, and it all starts with a conversation. Successful people feel good about what they do and build that feeling into their sales conversations.

I'd like to share a story about my dear friend and client who is a growth strategist. She helps entrepreneurs build to seven figures by developing programming and understanding their revenue streams. She has been a client of mine for over three years, and our client relationship really started one fateful day when we met for lunch.

She called me one day and sounded completely defeated. She said there had to be some kind of disconnect from what she was saying, because she wasn't experiencing success in her sales conversations. She asked to meet for lunch and discuss the issue. When I walked into the restaurant, she was sitting at the booth furthest from the front door. I sat next to her in the booth and could see the frustration and defeat in her eyes. I asked her to tell me what had happened. She told me that she wasn't a good salesperson and that she didn't know how to sell effectively. She had worked so hard at creating a brilliant business model with service offerings that were clear and specific, but something was missing.

I asked her to walk me through how she was selling. She told me she would invite people who showed a sincere interest in her to a call or face-to-face meeting to get to know one another. She would go over her service offerings with them when they showed interest. Her prospect would say something like, "This sounds incredible, but I need to think about it." She continued sharing how she would send them an email or call them in the next few days and get no response. My mind started to race and it became clear to me where the disconnect was: her prospects weren't ready to be sold to.

It may sound odd since the reaction she was getting from her prospects sounded positive. They took the appointment and even said that they were interested. Why weren't they buying? I looked her in the eye and shared where the first point of disconnect was: she needed separate meetings.

People who show interest in us at a networking event or from an introduction are looking to get to know us. They may know what we do, how we do it, and even what type of investment they need to make, but they don't know you yet. The first meeting you have with someone often needs to be around getting to know them and them getting to know you. Position your meeting as just that. Invite them for an opportunity to share who they are and you will do the same, no strings attached.

If they are interested in becoming a client or learning about what that looks like, they will ask buying questions. Buying questions are questions an interested person will ask in order to begin making a decision about working with you. Some examples of what they will ask include "So, what does it look like to work with you?" "How do people get started?" or "How much does it cost?" When they ask these questions, your natural instinct is to share that information right then and there. That is where my client was selling before her prospect was ready to be sold to. Think about it this way, you wouldn't ask someone to marry you after one date, right?! Instead of fully answering those questions you can answer them like this:

> *"Thank you for asking! I would love to share that with you. There is a range of ways that clients work with me, and I would be happy to go over that with you. But for the time being I want to protect our time and get to know one another. I typically set up a separate time to go over my service offerings and give you an opportunity to share what you are going through and see if I may be able to help."*

The separate meeting you will refer to is something like a free consultation or discovery session.

I shared this information with my client. Immediately, I could see the lightbulb go off for her. Her eyes welled a bit and she said, "It's SO simple." Most of this is; it's simple because you have to put yourself in your prospect's shoes.

There is a flow to your sales process that requires intentional communication. You need to know the process if you want your prospective client to work with you. Knowing what to offer them, and more importantly how to offer it to them, is the objective of a communication strategy. To that end, there are four phases of conversation in every business. You must have a sales process, follow-up strategy, client retention plan and existing client selling strategy. The sales process is the first communication strategy that helps you transition into the next phase of conversation.

One of the struggles with selling is that you need to gauge the readiness of your prospect. You need to understand their readiness to hear about how to work with you and their readiness to purchase. One of the worst things you can do is to make assumptions. Remember what assumptions do to you and your business? The best way to make it so you are working with facts instead is to know your sales process. The exercise below will help you establish separate meetings in your sales process that not only set your prospect up for being ready to be sold to, but put you in a position to sell.

Defining your sales process:
You first need to have separate meetings. Separating your meetings is important because each meeting sets a specific purpose and an intention to the process. Your sales process should follow these three steps:

1. A getting-to-know-you meeting

2. Introductory consultation

3. One of two things will happen at this step:
   a. They become a client
   b. They aren't ready to purchase
   (here's where the 8 Touch Follow-Up Strategy begins, see chapter twelve)

The getting-to-know-you meeting is strictly like it sounds: a time for you to get to know your prospect as an individual and for them to get to know you. Your prospects want to feel heard and know that they matter. In order to build a relationship that makes them feel comfortable, you must protect each meeting you have with them and be their guide through the process. Prospects will buy from you once they know you, trust you and like you! The key to these meetings is to have a set of questions to guide your conversation and uncover the information you need to better assess the situation of your prospect.

These questions in a getting-to-know-you meeting should look something like this:

1. **Ask them about their story.** "Tell me your story; I'd love to know how you came to be where you are!" This question gives your prospect a place to be heard. You are opening the door for them to share their past and present circumstances.

2. **Ask about their personal lives.** "Do you have a spouse? Children? Pets?" These questions make business personal. It allows your prospect to feel like they matter. It also allows them to feel that you aren't just having a meeting about business; you are actually getting to know them.

3. **Ask them a question that can reveal a common problem**

for the solution you offer. One of the best questions I can ask a prospect is, "How do you find your clients? Do you do a lot of networking?" The reason this question is important for me is that it often unveils the common problem of connecting with a lot of people through networking, but not having processes in place to build clients and relationships. Think about what that question could be for you. What is the question that could uncover a problem you have the answer to? Use the space below to brainstorm:

_____
_____
_____
_____
_____
_____
_____
_____

4. **Ask them a question that shows that you are listening and want to help.** "How can I support you?" This question often incites prospects to say what or who they are looking for. This is an opportunity for you to think of people to connect them to.

5. **Ask for the best way to refer them.** "What should I listen for to make an introduction for you?" Once again, this question makes them feel heard. Their answer will allow you to have a better understanding of who to introduce them to.

When you lead the conversation with your questions, you are establishing interest in your prospect. Take notes while they speak so you can add them to your CRM after your meeting and keep track of your conversations.

Not everyone is comfortable during the getting-to-know-you meeting. You may be one of those people. Having questions prepared is a way to break through awkward silences or not knowing what to say. If your prospect is being guided during the conversation and isn't asking many questions, that's okay. However, it does not mean that you spend the whole conversation talking about them. This is your opportunity for them to get to know you as well. If they have not reciprocated, don't assume that they aren't interested; they may just not know what to do. Be a good example for them, and once they are finished simply say, "Thank you for sharing this with me. May I share my story with you?"

If your prospect is interested in working with you in the getting-to-know-you-meeting, they will ask buying questions. As a recap, those questions look something like this:

"What does it look like to work with you?"

"How much does it cost to work with you?"

"How do people start working with you?"

These are wonderful questions! These questions allow you to set up your next step of the sales process. As I explained to my client, when someone asks you buying questions, give them a blanket answer and offer them the next step, like how I advised her to setup a separate meeting to review services.

If your prospect takes you up on the introductory consultation, you have successfully identified them as a qualified prospect.

An introductory consultation is an opportunity for your prospect to get a taste of what it's like to work with you without a financial obligation. Two beautiful things happen in this point of your sales process. When your prospect shows up for their introductory session, they are ready to be sold to and you have a right to sell. There are no assumptions here. Each party knows exactly why you are meeting and it is safe to have a conversation about how you can help them. Sounds pretty sweet, right?! This step is the game-changer that, once my client implemented it, solved the issue of sharing information at the wrong time.

Let's talk about what your introductory consultation should look like. This meeting is an opportunity for you to show them how you serve. It starts by having a questionnaire. This questionnaire should be something you send to them ahead of time and can review before you meet. The questionnaire should consist of questions that will help you identify their pain points and their level of readiness to work with you.

When developing your questionnaire, think about the problems you solve. Ask questions that are thought-provoking and open-ended. For example, the first entry in my questionnaire is, "What is your biggest communication challenge?" I then ask questions around each part of my program—about their sales process, follow-up strategy, client retention, and client selling. When I receive their questionnaire, I review their responses and have an inkling of the solution I can provide prior to our meeting.

Your sales process requires you to understand how you want your clients to work with you. For example, a client of mine is a creativity coach who offers business-strategy coaching by adding intentional creativity to clients' business objectives. She puts on local and international retreats and offers workshops and one-on-one sessions. Her ultimate objective is to get clients to attend retreats. Knowing that the main objective is to fill the retreats, her sales process addresses the steps it takes to guide her prospects to them.

We began by working on her messaging to give her audience a clear understanding of who she is, how she serves, and her ideal client. We then took that messaging and created the strategy for presenting it at a networking event, on her website, through one-on-one conversations, and in her social media campaigns. She now not only has the strategy, but the steps within that strategy to convert prospects into retreat-attending clients. Her sales process was defined by starting with the end goal in mind and working backwards to realize the steps it will take to convert a new prospect in to a retreat attendee.

The processes I have given you are a systematic way of guiding prospects through your sales process to your ultimate goal!

twelve.

YOU DON'T FOLLOW-UP

The importance of having a communication strategy is also to sell your services to the right audience. It allows you to stop wasting time because you don't know how you are going to build relationships with the people you meet.

Everyone knows that there is fortune in the follow-up, but how the hell do you get to that fortune without sounding like a sleazy salesperson? It's a feeling that keeps people from using the connections they make to build a prosperous business. Follow-up takes multiple touches, meaning multiple attempts at communicating with your prospect to get engagement. Did you know it usually takes five to seven touches before a prospect will take the next step in your sales process? Did you know that it takes multiple forms of communication to make up enough touches for that prospect to bite?

Lack of effective follow-up is the number-one killer of sales. All of my clients, without exception, found they were following up with prospects ineffectively. It gets overlooked, but if done effectively, follow-up can provide the greatest success. Realizing that you're not good at this can be a tough pill to swallow for any entrepreneur, especially if you have experienced previous success. Just remember, there's always room for improvement.

One particular client identified her lack of follow-up early on in her business. We started working together and found a solution for her through my 8 Touch Follow-Up strategy, which you will learn in detail later. Together, we focused on the problems her ideal client faced and presented those problems in a bold yet conversational manner. We identified the sales process she needed to lead her clients to work with her, and set the communication strategy to do its magic.

She followed the process and repeatedly had prospects move on to the next step of her sales process, usually between the fifth and eighth touch. 80 percent of conversions happen after the fifth touch. You may be wondering, why go to eight then? The answer is it gives you three more opportunities to get your prospect to engage. 93 percent of entrepreneurs give up after the second touch. Which one will you be?

A follow-up strategy also takes leadership. You must lead your prospect from one conversation to the next. Think of it this way: it's impossible to follow if you don't know how to lead. During your sales process, you are leading your prospect from one conversation to the next to get them comfortable with being sold to and you comfortable with selling. If they don't know what the next step looks like, they will decide what needs to happen by themselves. Those damn assumptions show up once again!

Your prospect may have objections. It could be that they currently aren't in a place to afford your services or the timing isn't right. There could be a multitude of reasons, but no matter what it is, it is now your responsibility to stay connected to them and to follow-up with them until they are ready.

I want you to imagine a table with two chairs. One chair is for a person who has a problem. The other chair is for the person with the solution to the problem. The conversation begins with the person with a problem sharing their pain points and their desire to fix the problem. The other person educates on how their solution can solve the problem and addresses each of the pain points. It's just a conversation.

That is sales. Simply an exchange of problems and solutions. Throughout our day, we are constantly on one side of the table or the other. When you are at a restaurant, your pain point or problem is that you are hungry. The server solves your hunger by bringing you food. This may seem like a trite example, but that's the point. The sales conversation is simple: it is an exchange of needs and solutions.

When you are on the solution side of the table, your sole responsibility is to educate your prospect on the solutions and effectively communicate the steps it takes to solve their problem.

Assuming that you have the solution to your prospect's problem is a dangerous place to be. This is why it is critical that you ask the right questions and guide them through the process. During your follow-up strategy, you will again be visited by negative head trash. You will make assumptions about why they had an objection and why they didn't purchase right away.

Don't allow the assumptions to take over. Trust the process and don't fall into the 93 percent category. When your prospect doesn't respond to you after one or two emails, you may start hearing this in your mind: "They've moved on. Don't bother them anymore." And "If they were interested, they would've said something. They must have found someone else to help them." Put it all aside—this negative chatter keeps you from moving forward. It keeps you from providing the solution to problems!

Here's what is really happening with your prospect. He or she has a million things to do. They have their own business, their own lives, their own emails to tend to and every other distraction coming their way. Think about your day-to-day. Have you ever missed an email? Have you ever said to yourself, "Oh, I know I need to get back to that person!" Of course, you have! Your prospect is no different. This is what you need to know about follow-up: until your prospect gives you a yes or a no, it's your responsibility to stay in front of them.

Your leadership is the key to correcting assumptions about the prospects you haven't gotten a yes or a no from. You need to lead them through the steps, all the way through, and give them the opportunity to connect with you. My process takes us all the way through eight touches. If you follow the system and stick to it, you will hear from your prospect and get the answer you need to on-board them as a client or to let them sail off in the ocean.

The 8 Touch Follow-up Strategy looks like this:

1. **Thank you card:** One to two days after meeting

2. **Email:** Three to five days after thank you card sent

3. **Phone Call:** Two weeks later

4. **Email:** One week later

5. **Phone:** Two weeks later

6. **Email:** One week later

7. **Mailed Item:** Two weeks later

8. **Breakup Email:** One week later

This follow-up strategy is golden. It can be used in every form of follow-up you need in your business. It keeps you in front of prospects who aren't ready to buy yet and gives you tools to reconnect with people in your database you haven't spoken to in awhile, to launch a new program or service, and even to connect with people you presented to as a speaker. It includes every opportunity you could care to pursue. This process allows you to position yourself as a resource and continue to build the knowledge and trust factors while nudging your prospect to strike up a conversation with you.

Your follow-up strategy should be built on the 90/10 rule. 90 percent of what you are sending out in email, saying on the phone, mailing, and so on should be resourceful, informative, and educational. The remaining 10 percent is left for you to share the next step. Another way of stating the 90/10 rule is this: 90 percent of your communication is not about you, it is about who you are communicating with and their needs! The 10 percent is where it becomes about you and how you help them in to the next phase of conversation.

You may be asking yourself now, what the hell do I say when I am sending emails and making those dreaded phone calls? The answer lies in your next step and the resources you share to make up your 90 percent.

To hit 90 percent, focus on educational resources and invitations. By providing resources, you will be in a position of real value. Think about the person you are wooing. Think about their interests and how you could help with different facets of their business. For example, if your prospect is an entrepreneur, you can share resources around building their business, dealing with entrepreneurial struggles, goal setting, or business growth. The importance of sharing a resource when you are in the follow-up phase is to position yourself as a helpful go-to person. This way, you'll be at the forefront of their minds. Finding resources to share with your audience may seem like a tricky feat at first. Go back to the exercises around identifying your ideal client—think about what you find interesting, inspiring, and motivating. If you haven't yet developed collaborative partners, which we talk about more in the next chapter, start with celebrities and experts in the industry. Use Oprah, Tony Robbins, Marie Forleo, and so on. All of these idols have videos, blogs, articles and more to share with your audience.

Aside from sharing resources with prospects, you can invite them somewhere. I am not saying ask them out for drinks or dinner; I'm talking about inviting them somewhere as a professional. Ask them to attend a networking group or business event where you can introduce them to other business owners. Be the hero; the connector. Everyone wants to go into a room where they know someone, especially if that someone can introduce them to the right people.

After sharing a resource, the 10 percent of the 90/10 rule comes into play. You now get to tell them about the next step they can take to work with you. This is where you invite them to a free consultation. Be transparent so they can be led easily. You want to tell them about how much time it will take, what the expectations are, and how to schedule time with you.

Start simple, with a thank-you card. When you send out a thank-you card, you need to keep it 100 percent appreciative. This is not the time to sell. Thank-you cards are meant to show gratitude. Thank your prospect for spending time with you, reference your time together, and leave it at that. It doesn't have to be anything fancy. And for the love of God, please don't ask for referrals at this time! Everyone knows that you want referrals. You don't need to include a sticker or write a sentence about how much you appreciate referrals. We all do. Now is not the time to ask for them. However, it is appropriate to give them your business card.

After the initial card, you should move on to an email. For these, I want you to forget everything you've been programmed to do and stop using the phrases that are killing your business. Remove these from your vocabulary immediately:

- "I'm following-up…"
- "I'm checking in…"
- "I'm reaching out…"
- "I'm touching base…"

Get rid of them. Don't speak them, don't write them, and don't use them in your subject line. It is very likely that you have used these phrases before, if not today. These phrases may seem straightforward; and like they are describing your reason for connecting. In actuality, they are killing your business and deterring your prospect from connecting with you. Why? Put yourself in your prospect's shoes. When you receive an email with a subject line "Follow-up," the first thing you think is, "They want to sell me." No one wants that, and I don't want that for you!

So, here's how you replace that verbiage. Do not write a subject line in your email until you have written the body of the email. Take a sentence from your email and add it as your subject line. It could look something like this: "It was great meeting you" or "Thank you for your time." Once you get out of the habit of using meaningless phrases, your communication will become more intriguing and direct enough to lead your prospect in to the next step.

Another important factor to the 8-Touch Strategy is that it involves multiple forms of communication. You're giving multiple ways for your prospect to connect with you. It is important to mix it up a bit because if you use only one form of communication, you miss opportunities to meet prospects on their own turf. You can't assume that just because it's most comfortable for you to communicate one way, that your prospect communicates the same way.

You might be wondering, what about social media? Can you use social media as a point of connection in this strategy? The answer is yes. However, if you haven't proven your system yet or haven't been consistent in following one, I urge you to start with the one I provided. You can mix it up when you find your groove. Don't reinvent the wheel just yet.

In addition to opening the door to more interaction, your follow-up strategy allows you to keep an eye on where your prospects are in the buying process. Implementing any strategy comes down to being organized. Now the real benefit of a CRM comes in to play—you should be able to track your follow-up steps in the CRM. Record which step you are on, the message you sent or communicated, and set a reminder for yourself for when to implement the next step of the strategy. I know it may sound tempting to just remember where you are in the strategy. Seems simple enough to follow, right? Well my friend, that's where the trouble sets in: we can't remember everything.

Using your CRM to keep tabs on where you are in the process will keep you efficient and keep the strategy effective. This is also where it becomes imperative that you break up your time. You need to block out time to dedicate to follow-up and sales activities. Here are the top best practices when dedicating time these activities:

- Schedule time in your calendar; this is non-negotiable time

- Start with 30-minute increments

- The best days for follow-up activities are Tuesday,

Wednesday and Thursday

- The best times for follow-up are between 9:00 and 11:00 am and 2:00 and 4:00pm

- Use your CRM to organize your follow-up and stick to the strategy

One of the most important pieces of advice I can give you about follow-up is that it is never too late. It is never too late to start the conversation again. You need to give yourself some grace if you take more time between steps.

The steps are there as a guide, but life happens. You can get distracted and things can come up that mess up your schedule. I give you permission to pick up where you left off. The great part is that no one but you knows what should happen next and when. So don't worry if you fall of the wagon. We are talking about mind-shifts and the formation of new habits—it will take time, so be kind to yourself while you get the hang of it.

You have to do the work. Yes, you. Commonly, entrepreneurs are told to outsource whatever is not their "genius." Sales and follow-up may fall in to that category. However, these are fundamental skills that you must learn yourself. As a wise friend of mine once told me, "No one will ever sell your services better than you." I couldn't agree more. You need to roll-up your sleeves and learn these skills, implement the strategies, and see the benefits of having a process. Until you do, you won't be able to direct someone else how to do them for you.

thirteen.

YOU DON'T HAVE
COLLABORATIVE PARTNERS

Part of the 90/10 rule involves being a resource and sharing useful information. One of the best ways to showcase yourself as a resource to your audience is to surround yourself with collaborative partners. Collaborative partners are people who share the same ideal client as you and have a complimentary service to offer to that audience. Collaborative partners should be made up of people you trust implicitly to treat your clients the way you would treat them.

Developing your collaborative partners takes time. They are like best friends—you can't have a hundred. You want to look for building between three and five collaborative relationships.

Having collaborative partners allows you to share relevant content, resources, blogs, and videos with your audience that come directly from businesses that can serve them. You want to use your collaborative partners by sharing their content within your communications. In your follow-up strategy you need to share resources, so why not use resources from businesses you would directly refer your prospects and clients to anyway? Here's what building collaborative partners does for your business:

- You are no longer alone. You can stay within your expertise and be able to refer out business to your partners.

- You look like a hero to your prospects and clients. They don't have to do the searching to find the right person for them.

- You can and should leverage your partnerships to get in front of their prospects and clients.

- You have a go-to company. You become a one-stop shop for your audience and whether they work with you immediately or down the road you are top of mind.

- You can stop the hustle for clients. Building collaborative partnerships allows for you to build a business that runs on referral. We all want that, right? The bonus here is that these prospects are already coming preapproved and qualified to be an ideal client.

Another reason why collaborative partners are essential to your business has to do with you. There is one thing that I attribute the success of my business to more than any other factor: my collaborative partners. I use them for my own business as well as sending them to my clients. We all know it takes a village to raise a family, right? Same goes for being a successful business owner. There can be some barriers to break down and through when accepting this fact. You can't do this alone. I repeat, YOU CANNOT DO THIS ALONE.

Running a successful business takes leadership, ownership, accountability, recognition of mistakes, compromises, and sometimes eating huge pieces of humble pie. You have a lot of pride as an entrepreneur and see your business as your baby. Why would you let anyone else close to your baby? Let alone babysit or, even scarier, give input as to how to raise your baby? Let me tell you.

1. You are your own biggest roadblock.
How many times have you spent WAY too much time creating a project, process or system for your business? You spin your wheels, get frustrated and end up with a half-finished project. This is why collaboration and having a village of your own comes in handy. You need your collaborative partners to be people you trust to help create, brainstorm and critique your ideas. This has to be a safe space and these must be people you trust. You wouldn't put them in front of your clients if you didn't trust them with your own business, right?

2. You don't know everything, and that's OKAY!
I know, I know. Sometimes we feel like we should have all the answers around our own businesses. It is our baby, right? Shouldn't we innately know how to answer all questions or problems that arise? Absolutely not. Your village is meant to provide you with collaborative experiences and expertise. You can shed light on their dilemmas and they can shed light on yours.

2. Sometimes things suck.
I can't say it more plainly. This shit is HARD. You must be on your A game every day, all day. You need to show up at networking events with a smile and an attitude that everything is 100 percent A-Okay. Well, let's be real. Sometimes it isn't! Sometimes you run into problems you had no idea existed. As an entrepreneur, you are faced with a plethora of challenges and obstacles. This is why your village is so important. These are talking-you-off-the ledge, keep-you-from-quitting, kick-you-in-the-ass kind of situations. You need to allow your village to pump you up and push you back in the ring.

Collaborative partners are the pillar of a successful business. They serve your own business just as much as they serve the clients you help. If you align yourself with other successful businesses and can serve their clients, it's a win-win partnership. Be patient, it takes time!

fourteen.

YOUR CLIENTS DON'T HEAR FROM YOU

We've talked about how your business relationships are similar to your personal ones. Well, now is when the hard part of customer relationship management sets in. Just like a marriage, you need to keep the love alive. You've spent time and effort ensuring a rockin' experience while wooing your prospect and then delivering your services, so you can't stop now! In order to earn the trust needed to gain referrals and continue to earn their business, you must stay in front of clients and keep them happy.

> 68 percent of clients who leave do so because they don't feel appreciated.

Your communication strategy needs to continue even after you have earned their business. Once they become a client, you need to communicate appreciation and acknowledgement to keep the relationship going. Remember, people want to know that they matter and they're being heard. Giving your clients a voice by asking about their needs is the foundation of a long-lasting relationship.

A client of mine owns a cleaning business. She and her husband work very hard to go above and beyond for their clients. She came to me because she wanted to be outstanding in the industry; she wanted to do something her competitors weren't. We focused on a strategy for her staying in front of her clients, a client-retention plan that allowed her to stay engaged with her clients and drive repeat business and referrals. Their main strategy needed to provide unexpected appreciation and recognition.

Retention begins by being proactive and mapping out a plan that can be implemented easily. A common concern my clients have is "I am focused on getting new clients, so I will worry about client retention when I have a lot of people." This is a backwards approach. The second that you start your business, you should have a plan for retaining your clients. All it takes is one client to start building an empire. So whether you are just starting out or you're in the middle of building, it's time to get intentional about keeping your clients happy.

The first place to start is by creating an outline of what you're going to share with your clients throughout the year. The messaging you create will be dispersed using multiple forms of communication so you reach your client where they are.

Think about the things you like and that matter to you most. Revisit the persona exercise. The clients you have attracted and will continue to attract have the same values. When communicating with your clients, you want to share relevant information and other things that continue to build your relationships with them. The exercise below will guide you through identifying what you can talk about and share with your client base.

In the chart below, brainstorm ideas on subject matter you can share with your client base. This will be used in emails, social media posts, gifts for clients, phone calls, and other communications.

Months of the Year	Subject matter: Likes, Favorite Holidays, Community Events, Hobbies	Service Offerings
Write out the months of the year	Example: Dogs Fourth of July MaxFund Animal Shelter Fundraiser Cocktail bars	Example: One-on-one consulting Group workshops

Once you've finished this exercise, I want you to assign a subject matter and service offering to each month of the year. Then you can create a messaging guide. A messaging guide will become an outline you can use to create content for emails, social media posts, and so on. To fill out your messaging guide, you'll need to put your creative hat on. The elements of the messaging guide are as follows:

Personal piece: A resource you can share that gives insight into something you enjoy personally.

Community piece: An event or recognition of a charity, organization, or even another business you want to support and bring awareness to.

Service piece: This is your 10 percent. Share what you are focusing on selling for that quarter. This is a subtle reminder to your clients of what you can help them with.

Monthly message: Get creative. Use your personality. If you are bit sassy like I am, make it sassy. If you are funny, use humor. If you are stuck, use the seasons to provide you with some ammo for messaging.

Sample Messaging Guide

Quarter example for CR Conversations:
January – February – March
Month – January

Personal piece: Example – Top cocktail bars to visit in Denver

Community piece: Example – MaxFund Animal Shelter Adoption event

Service piece: Example – The quickie strategy session
Monthly message (subject line for email): Baby it's cold outside! Time for a quickie...

Now you try...

Month:

_____

Personal piece:

_____

Community piece:

_____

Service piece:

_____

Monthly message (subject line for email):

_____

Month:

_____

Personal piece:

_____

Community piece:

_____

Service piece:

_____

Monthly message (subject line for email):

_____

While you create this messaging guide, think about something you would be drawn to make you open in an email or like on a social media post. This can be challenging and will take some time. Start with one quarter at a time. This can be an email you send to your database or a monthly blog or social media post. The purpose for doing this is to share something fun, engaging, and resourceful with your audience each month.

Where do we go from here? Great question. You can now use this guide to proactively stay in front of your clients. The next thing to do is to create emails, preferably in your CRM, that can be scheduled to go out to your list. You can put it in a newsletter format with a structure and images or keep it loosey-goosey and just write a standard email. Just add a couple of sentences about each of the pieces you have planned out. You want to stick to the 90/10 rule like you do in your follow-up strategy. Leave your service piece for the end. That's your 10 percent.

The next phase of creating a client retention plan is the old-school personal touches. I'm talking about phone calls and thank-you cards. Each quarter, you should send a thank you card, preferably handwritten, to each of your top clients. Yes, I said top clients. You don't need to send a card to each and every person who has come through your business. Most of my clients have what we call a top 50 category. These are 50 of their best clients. They define "best" as people they truly love working with; who currently give referrals or would be open to giving them; the ones that most obviously value their service. Once you have your top 50 defined—and you might only have one person in there right now—send them a thank-you card and pick up the phone to tell them you appreciate them. That's it. It doesn't have to be a long conversation and it most definitely doesn't involve selling anything.

The best feeling in the world is getting someone on the phone and hearing the pause on the other end after you say, "I am just calling to thank you and tell you that you are appreciated." You'll find that it leaves them dumbfounded. No one calls just to say thank you. There's always an ulterior motive. Hearing them say, "THANK YOU! That's really nice!" is a beautiful thing.

The final piece of a client retention plan is giving them a gift. We all wish we could shower our clients with luxurious spa days, steak dinners, and fancy bottles of wine. This just isn't the reality for most. So how do you convey the feeling that the fancy stuff provides without breaking the bank? Easy. You send them a small gift once per quarter at unexpected times, and they will be equally delighted! Sounds great, right?
One of the easiest ways to create gifts for your clients is to hit up the dollar store and pop over to Pinterest for a few minutes. Pinterest is a wonderful place to find ideas for client gifts, and the dollar store is a cost-effective place to find gifts for as many people as you can. It really is the thought that counts. Some examples of gifts I have sent to clients from my Pinter-est-and-dollar-store combo:

Bubbles and scratch tickets with a card that says, "We're blown away by how lucky we are to have you!"

Wildflower seed packets with a note saying, "You are the seeds to our blooming business and for that, we thank you!"

The gift does not need to be grandiose. It just needs to be heartfelt!

You now have a combination of touches that your client can see, hear and feel. They will learn more about you, fall deeper in love with you, and feel all warm and fuzzy with appreciation! Your client retention plan will consist of the following:

- Once per month, they get an email

- You will post on social media at least 3 times per week

- Quarterly, your top 50 clients get a thank-you card

- Quarterly, your top 50 clients get a phone call

- Twice a year, your top 50 clients get a gift

Back to my carpet-cleaning client. Once she created and implemented her client-retention strategy, she uncovered dozens of repeat business opportunities and renewed relationships with her existing clients. This resulted in more referrals and increased revenue. Your existing client base is like those business cards: a goldmine. You just need to start digging. A good client retention plan will allow you to be proactive and open the door for business growth.

Remembering the new golden rule, you need to remember that your clients are humans, not a business. I stress this because we can be so quick to forget it when we are lost in the delivery of our services, the operation of our businesses, and the stresses of being a business owner. We need to be reminded.

A simple, immediately implementable strategy to keeping your clients top-of-mind and feeling appreciated as individuals is to remember important dates. These dates could be birthdays, business anniversaries, or even the anniversary of their engagement with you.

You can communicate to your clients that you recognize their special day. You can incorporate promotions tied to their birthday or anniversary, send a handwritten note, or feature them in your communication. No matter which way you choose, you must have a system to store AND remind you of these important dates. This is yet another time that I am adamant about having a

CRM. Use it to keep on top of your clients' important dates.

We've already talked about the importance of making a good first impression, but there is even more to be said about maintaining and exceeding your first impression. I am a huge advocate of and participant in continuing education and training to improve upon sales practices, operations and processes, and, of course, client service. It is imperative that you continue to learn about ways to better serve your clients. Continue to strive for excellence and implement processes that create an exceptional experience for your clients every time they interact with you.

One of the best ways to provide exceptional service is to continue the good experience for your client no matter who they deal with during or after the service is provided. If you have employees or use your collaborative partners during your services, introduce them to your clients so they get to know each person in your operation. If you create a culture of exceptional client service that involves your staff and partners—even by using simple introductions—you will see a significant change in how your clients interact with your company by their increased loyalty and comfort.

Yes, I said it again and will continue to remind you. In our current culture, we have seen a pretty drastic shift in how consumers interact with businesses. Not only has consumerism moved us, but we have shifted in the way we interact socially. A great deal of human connectivity has been lost over the past decade due to technology. These changes have made us more comfortable with sending a Facebook message than picking up the phone to call someone. That being said, a cultural shift is emerging: people are craving human interaction. They want to receive physical mail versus email, and most importantly, people want to be heard and know they matter.

The impact you can make on your relationship with your clients and in your community directly influences how we interact as a culture. When you remember that your clients are human beings with desires, fears, and worries that they want to be heard, you can increase your service to a level that virtually exceeds any online interaction. You will know that you are influencing your clients when you see them smile, when you hear it in their voice, and when you see them coming back to have that feeling again and again.

Now that you've put together a strategy for keeping your clients in love with you, it's time to talk about what you have earned—the right to ask for testimonials and referrals. Many people tend to ask for referrals after they've met someone for the first time. That's basically like asking a first date if they'd like to introduce you to their sibling because you're more interested in them. Yuck. Or worse, they don't ask for referrals at all. As for testimonials, many people shy away from them entirely. It feels uncomfortable to ask someone to say nice things about you. I get it, it feels self-involved, but my friend, it's time to shake that mindset once again and ask for what you need!

There is a beautiful synchronicity between testimonials and referrals: with the first comes the second. You've shown your clients that you appreciate them, they've engaged with you, and feel like they're on top of the world thanks to your careful delivery. Now is the time to ask them for a testimonial.

A testimonial is representation of their experience that you can share with the world! However, people often give a personal testimonial, something along the lines of, "Oh it was so wonderful to work with Katie, she's so nice!" Well, as lovely and flattering as that is, it sure as shit doesn't say anything about what it's like to work with Katie. As I said before, it's impossible to follow if you don't know how to lead, right? The same goes for collecting testimonials. People need you to tell them what you want from them. Give them guidelines for a testimonial that you can share with others that will give a prospect an idea of what it was like to work with you. Below is my formula for collecting money-making testimonials:

You need to guide your client into giving you a testimonial that explains what it was like to work with you and the benefit they received by doing so. You want to ask your clients to answer three questions:

1. What problem led you to work with me?

2. What solution did you receive as a result of working with me?

3. What words would you use to describe what it was like to work with me?

The testimonial should look something like this:

"I was having trouble staying connected and following up with people I met when networking, and that's what lead me to work with Katie. After working with Katie, I now have the strategies and steps to be organized and never miss an opportunity to connect with a prospect. Working with Katie is strategic, deliberate, fun, and brings results."

That's a much better testimonial than "Katie is nice." Using the formula above, you will be able to attract prospects by helping them identify with clients you have already helped. It gives them something to relate to, and something they can create expectation around.

Now for the referral. Your client has delivered a perfectly plated, yummy testimonial. Thank them for it, and at the same time ask them for a referral.

You want to be specific and intentional with your ask. Have you ever kicked yourself for missing an opportunity to ask for a referral? I feel ya. We can beat ourselves up when we don't ask for referrals.

Back to when I was selling life insurance, I would start out with a list of leads. Then, in every single house I was in, I would collect at least ten referrals. TEN REFERRALS out of every house! I got to thinking, why was it so easy to get referrals to sell life insurance when it felt like pulling teeth to ask for referrals in a service-based business?

Well, my friend, I figured it out. It all comes down to two things: timing and the ask. When I was selling insurance and asking for referrals of other people to present to I was specific, clear, concise and HAD EARNED the right to ask for the referral.

Let's explore each of these a bit deeper, shall we:

1. Timing.

There is always an appropriate time to ask for referrals. The key is being able to identify when it is appropriate. Each of our businesses has a sales cycle. You must pay attention to the amount of time you spend with your clients for a service. As stated before, after you collect a stellar testimonial, you have earned the right to ask for a referral.

2. The Ask.

Now that you have received a testimonial from your client,

you have the RIGHT to ask for a referral. Your client has es-
tablished that you provided them with a solution and they are
happy. You now need to take their testimonial and turn it into
an ask. Three components they have given you can be turned
into a referral request:

- They expressed their pain points
- They explained how you provided a solution to those
  pain points
- They have identified themselves as an ideal client

4. The Ask, Part Two.

Just like your 30-second commercial when networking, you
need to be specific about how you are asking for referrals.
DO NOT use words like "anyone," "anybody," or "someone
who." You must be specific. Ask your client for an introduction to a (however they identify themselves): busy business
owner, solo entrepreneur, sales manager or employer. Then
add in the pain points. "I would like an introduction to a solo
entrepreneur like yourself who is experiencing (pain points)
that I can help serve by providing (outline the solution in their
words)."

5. The Ask, Part Three.

Once you formulate the messaging and specify your ask, you
must direct your client to provide the referral in your favor. We
get to the halfway mark and make the ask, but then we weenie
out and say, "Have them give me a call." Um, no. No, no, no.
You need to lead the referrer to make an equally warm email
introduction. Asking for an email introduction between you and
the person they are referring is a non-threatening equal opportunity for you and the referred to get to know one another.

fifteen.

YOU STOP LEADING
AFTER THE SALE

After you've sold, your communication strategy continues; the conversation with your client isn't over. It is time to think about how you're going to continue to serve your clients. How do you keep them coming back for more, and what is the more they are able to receive? This is another situation where you need to have the next step in mind. Just like how you guide a prospect through your sales process and follow-up strategy, you must always be prepared to share the next step with them. This means that you need to know exactly what to offer them next, how to offer it to them, and how to find out what they need. You need to keep an eye on them and their business needs.

Your clients look to you for guidance, not just the initial solution to their problem. You have built a relationship on trust and you have become a resource to them. You are their advocate and they will look to you for advice on continuing their business success.

One of the best ways to find out what your client needs is to simply ask them. You can do this in a few ways. You can send a survey to your clients; you can send out individual emails; you can pick up the phone and have a conversation—whatever is most comfortable and convenient for you. Personally, I like to ask my clients when I see them in-person. To this end, each year I do what I call a gratitude event. Who doesn't like a party? Putting together a little shindig for your customers is an excellent way to show your appreciation for them and an excellent time to receive feedback.

I advise you to use your customers as resources: When looking for a location, think about customers who have brick-and-mortar businesses that might work for a party location. Your customer will most likely be delighted to host an event at their location because it gives them free advertising to your customer base and their guests.

Another great way to make the most out of your gratitude event and use your money-making testimonials is to get it on film. Have someone (not you) take short, one- or two-minute video testimonials from your guests. This is going to increase excitement about your business and give you the opportunity to use their testimonials for marketing at a later date.

During the party, I give each attendee a small gift, a thank-you card, and have them fill out a sheet of paper with two questions on it: "How has your business evolved?" and "What is the biggest need you have currently?" By asking these questions, I get insight in to what my clients need right here and now. They could need a vendor or have a problem they need help solving. Their businesses grow and develop needs for contractors or staff or new territories. I collect their surveys and determine if my services meet their needs.

Business evolution can come in two forms. It could be that you need to provide additional support, perhaps a workshop or another consulting option. It could be that you need to connect them with collaborative partners, or incorporate something new into your own service offerings. By knowing how to evolve and meet your client's needs, you'll know how to best serve them.

Asking for this type of feedback makes your client feel that they matter. It takes another mindset-shift of no longer treating your interactions with your clients as transactions, but as a relationship. Relationships are ongoing. They take effort and need your attention.

There are additional ways to keep your clients feeling the love and wanting to evolve with you. The first way is to follow them. I don't mean for you to get all creepy and start following them in detective attire, staring at them from behind a newspaper at their favorite coffee shop. I mean on social media. You want to get to know your customers and find out their likes and dislikes. What bring joy to their lives? What books, articles, and blogs are they reading?

When you ask to be Facebook friends with your customers, add them on LinkedIn, or follow them on Twitter or Pinterest, you are building a new level of your relationship with them. Please heed my advice, though, when I say to always remain professional! You must be conscious of what you are adding to your social media because your customers will be following you just as you are following them.

Evolving your business to align with your clients is a combination of keeping them in love with you, helping them feel appreciated, and ensuring that they feel like they are heard. By appreciating them while also asking what their needs are, you will continue to build a relationship that will prove to be lucrative and prosperous.

Listening to the needs of your customers allows you to deliver the services they need. You must be able to serve clients in multiple ways, from an entry-level offering to the most comprehensive service package you can offer. The best way to look at your service offerings is to think about the different ways food can be served and how many options you can receive. You can view your service offerings like appetizers, an entree, and a buffet.

An entry-level offering should be like an appetizer. It is enough to satiate their hunger, but leaves them wanting more. Your appetizer offering could be a do-it yourself course, your book, or an introductory consulting or coaching session. It should allow them to get a taste of what you do. Your appetizer is meant for people that are trying you out, who may not know what problems they have and don't fully understand their needs yet. Done right, they'll realize they were hungrier than they thought.

Your next level of service offerings is like an entree. It's a middle-of-the-road offering. You know that they are going to get hungry again, but an entrée-sized offering will give them what they need and keep them full until their next meal. This offering should be a full serving of what you offer. You don't give them everything, but you give them enough to feel full while they put what you've taught them into practice.

An entree offering should deliver exactly what they need at that time. This could be a four-hour consulting or coaching session, a virtual training series in a group, or a workshop. They will have plenty to think about, homework to complete, and things to implement. But there should still be room for more learning. That's where the buffet comes in.

Your final offering is a combination of appetizers, entrees and everything else your client's heart could desire. Everything you can offer them is on the table—the ultimate primo package. You want to pack it full of time with you, advanced learning options, and incorporate what you offer on the appetizer and entree level. This is also an opportunity for you to include your collaborative partners in the package.

As an example, my highest level includes full access to The Core Conversations program, hands-on, one-on-one training, and one hour of paid time with each of my collaborative partners. All the experts I have aligned myself with are included in this package so my client has the opportunity to work on all aspects of their business at once. It's a CR Conversations all-you-can-eat deal.

For help with creating offering levels and how to serve them to your clients, use the space below to identify them:

Appetizer: Example for CR Conversations – Talk it Out Tuesday. This is a free training I do every Tuesday in short snippets via Facebook Live.

_____

_____

_____

_____

Entree: Example for CR Conversations – The Conversation Club. This is a low-cost entry point to an online membership with live and recorded trainings, a Facebook group, and training from additional experts.

_____

_____

_____

_____

Buffet: Example for CR Conversations – The Nitty Gritty, one-on-one consulting that includes access to all the above offerings. It is the most intensive option and clients get the most access to me and my partners. Plus, they receive The Conversation Club and my Talk it out Tuesday videos.

_____

_____

_____

_____

Be sure to incorporate your collaborative partners! By doing so, you become a one-stop shop. After all, it can be difficult for entrepreneurs to get access to all the experts they need help from. Make it easy for your clients to get what they need when they need it and in a way that makes them feel comfortable. Setting up your offerings in this way makes it easy to continue to sell.

sixteen.

YOU DON'T CONTINUE TO SELL

Now that you have different levels of service, you can continue to sell to clients beyond the initial engagement. You are once again at the sales table. It is your job to see if your client has any additional problems that need solving.

There are two sales terms that are applicable when it comes to continued customer selling. The first is upselling. Upselling involves upgrading prospects to the next level after selling them something smaller. For example, a client who chose your appetizer level as their entry point and decides to buy an entrée has been upsold.

The second term is cross-selling. Cross-selling is when you sell your customer an additional service while they are currently working with you in one capacity, or selling them two offerings at once. For example, you may have multiple DIY courses for your clients to purchase. Instead of your client needing just one of your appetizers, they may need a few or all of them. By having multiple DIY options to choose from, you can cross-sell multiple services at one time.

Understanding these terms and crafting strategies around them is imperative if you want to gain repeat revenue from your existing customers. When you listen to their needs and adapt your offerings to meet those needs, you have an everlasting opportunity to serve your customers. In the coaching and consulting realm, there are always big opportunities for repeat business. Your clients can re-take parts of your program when they need refreshers. You can also bundle your offerings to give them the most bang for their buck. For example, if you are hosting a workshop, you could bundle your DIY training as a bonus offering. This can be an effective sales tactic that helps your clients feel they are getting exceptional value.

The ways to communicate upselling or cross-selling to your clients comes in a few forms. The first comes during their contract renewal or at the end of their initial service. You will want to set up time to go through the process of completing their work with you and find an appropriate time to talk to them about next steps. Secondly, you can go back to clients who have worked with you in the past and introduce customer-exclusive offerings, up to and including discounts.

Let's talk about contract renewal. About 30 days from the end of your service, you want to set up a closing session. You want this session to be in-person or done with virtual chat such as Zoom or Skype so you can see your client's body language. This is because any time you are selling, it's best to get every sense of their reception to your conversation. In this meeting, you want to have a goal. Be strategic and come up with some sort of exit questionnaire.

Your questionnaire should have questions like:

- What was your biggest take away from working together?

- Where were you at the beginning of our work? How do you feel now?

118

- In our work together, has there been anything that wasn't covered that you would like to address?

- In our work together, did you discover additional needs for your business? If so, what are they?

- What do you feel are the next steps?

By asking these questions you are allowing them to set the context around your next steps. They will let you know if they need more, and what their experience was like working with you. Given that you delivered exactly what you'd promised, there should be an opportunity to discuss where you feel their next steps are as well. Through these questions, you gain the opportunity to comfortably and confidently discuss what additional options you can offer. You must continue to give your clients a voice, listen to their needs, and lead with their best intentions in mind. It is your responsibility to educate your clients on the next step, whether it involves continuing together or if you'd advise them to work with one of your collaborative partners.

Having the final meeting to review next steps completes your sales cycle with your client. Now it's time to lather, rinse, and repeat, baby! Just remember: each time your customer invests in you, you need to continue to appreciate them and to stay in front of them during and post-service. Inviting them to a closing session will position you to assess their next steps each and every time. And throughout this entire process, you have shown them that they matter and given them the space to be heard.

seventeen.

YOU DON'T DO THE WORK

Every strategy we have talked about requires you to roll up your sleeves and get it done. You've read the strategies, done the exercises, and you have what you need. But now it's time to do it! The strategy part is easy enough, and it may be tempting to hand it off to someone else to implement.

Here is where I caution you: a client of mine came to me because she was struggling with the strategy of her sales process and follow-up. Each system we went through, every worksheet and every exercise was completed while we were in my office.

However, she ran into roadblocks. After each session, she was given homework. It was time to do the work we created a strategy for. I instructed her to create her database, implement the follow-up strategy and do the work. She kept running into obstacles. The head trash and desire to do everything else tugging at her attention instead of what made money got in her way.

The strategies I have given you are meant for you to build relationships and yes, makes you money! If you create the strategies but don't implement them, you have wasted your time. These strategies will bring you failure, not fortune, unless you implement them.

When you have implemented the strategies yourself, you will know how they need to be carried out and what you can expect the results to be. You will know how to navigate your CRM, what steps need to happen for follow-up, and what needs to be communicated to your customers for retention and appreciation. At this point, and only at this point, you can hand it off to an assistant or professional service to support you. You have to know how to guide them through your sales process just like you would a prospect, and how you want your company to be portrayed.

When hiring out a vendor or using an employee, you must keep these things in mind:

- **Your core values:** Make sure the people helping to implement these strategies know what you stand for and can represent you the way you would represent yourself.

- **Your process:** You must share your full strategy and the steps it takes to effectively communicate your sales conversations. I highly urge you to keep the closing of the sale for yourself. Remember, no one can sell your services like you can! The steps leading up to the sales conversation can be outsourced as long as you know the expectations.

Don't go completely hands-free: You still need to take the pulse of what's happening with your prospects and clients. Be sure to get reports and have whoever is helping you make notes in your CRM. This way you won't look like a ding-a-ling if someone assisting in the process has a conversation with a prospect or client. You will want the details of the last communication or interaction.

Hire only specialty services: Just like hiring coaches, you need to be sure the people who help implement your strategies are skilled in the art of human interaction and sales. They need to be personable, good on the phone and have your best interests in mind! For recommendations of specialty services, visit the partners page on my website, crconversations.com/Partners/.

Phone calls, emails, your database, staying in front of your clients, and returning to the sales table again and again—these all require your effort. I know it sucks. It's not the sexiest part of being an entrepreneur, but the people you serve need you! You can't help them if you don't communicate with them.

eighteen.

THE FORTUNE

Phew! There it is, The Core Conversations. From first contact through the closing session, you now have the tools you need to communicate strategically. Your sales conversations are no longer scary because there is a process behind them. You know what to say and when to say it. You have identified the reasons the F-word is entering your sales conversations, and you know what steps to take to turn it around. You have everything you need to successfully take prospects through your sales cycle and transition them into lifelong customers who continue to work with you and tell all their friends they need you! Feels pretty good, right?

Don't get me wrong, I know that hard work is involved and that nothing will happen overnight. Honestly, it shouldn't. This program takes time, dedication, and often a swift kick in the ass to keep going. Setup, thought, and deliberate action are all required to make this happen. Take it one step at a time and be kind to yourself. Give yourself some grace and know that everything will come together.

Your prospects are waiting for you. They need you. It's up to you to tell them how you can help and to be their guide. Set up your sales table and be the solution they need! You need to put yourself out there and be a bit vulnerable, but with a layer of crazy confidence. You are the expert. You know you can help. You have the strategy to effectively communicate your message and draw people into having a conversation with you. After all, that's all this is...just a conversation.

My own story of failing and finding the fortune that comes from rectifying mistakes gives you proof of how these strategies will help you. Miscommunication and not showing appreciation are killers. They kill your relationships, and those habits carry over into your work.

Don't make the same mistakes; be thoughtful and intentional with your conversations. Check to be sure you are communicating with kindness and understanding. Check that you are making your partners and prospects feel heard and that they matter. If you stop and take a breath before you fire off an email or use language that is inauthentic and generic and ask yourself how you would feel when receiving that message, you will be the person your customer needs you to be.

Follow the process and trust it. This shit works if you put in the effort and stick to the steps. Don't only do some of them, you won't get the most out of the strategy. So here's to you, your success, and showing that F-word who's boss!

THE NEXT STEP

Now that you have finished Fortune is in the Failure, you are ready to own the failures that are keeping you from moving forward. You've identified them. Now it's time to take action and do the work. The good news is, you aren't alone and you don't have to sell alone. There are thousands of entrepreneurs just like you who are struggling to find the fortune in their sales conversations.

You have the tools you need to get started, but there is more for you to tap in to. You need support, community and ongoing training. Just reading this book won't make the register ring. You have to revisit these strategies and continue to get training. So here's what you do now: join the club!

The Conversation Club is an online membership that allows you to continue getting the training and support you need to be successful!

THE CONVERSATION CLUB

Nobody likes failing. It pretty much sucks, especially when it comes to making money. We only want success, am I right? Success is sexy and something we all strive for! Success takes practice, purpose and sometimes a swift kick in the ass, especially when it comes to sales. I have created the Conversation Club as a community for hustlin' entrepreneurs to have consistent access to the sales training they need to reach the success they deserve. Sales will forever be a part of your business, so why only get sales training once?

Here's the deal-e-o:

Access to current and future Monthly Conversation Trainings
- The last Tuesday of every month at 4:00pm-5:00pm MST
- Zoom video chat hosted LIVE and recorded for future refreshing
- Each month is a new topic with juicy tidbits to keep your sales senses tingling

Monthly Open Office Hours
- Sometimes you just need someone to talk to
- One hour each month, the third Tuesday of every month, 4:30 – 5:30PM MST
- Submit your questions ahead of time and get LIVE answers to your questions
- Office hours are recorded so you can go back to them at any time
- Don't have a question to submit? All questions are answered with an audience just in case you need to hear it too

Private Facebook Group

We can't do this alone!
- Access to The Conversation Club Facebook Group
- Get to know other entrepreneurs that are in the same boat
- Share ideas
- Encourage one another
- Ask questions
- Find those that will help you continue your badassery

BONUS trainings with CR Conversations' Collaborative Strategists: Once per quarter, there will be an additional 60-minute live training done by one our Collaborative Strategists:

- Branding expert – Donna Galassi with Blue Zenith bluezenith.com
- Creativity Coach – Jacki Cox with Swirls swirlsllc.com
- Growth Strategist – Kimberly Alexander with Kimberly Alexander Inc. kimberlyalexanderinc.com
- Social Media expert – Hollie Clere with The Social Media Advisor thesocialmediaadvisor.com

Investment:

You have choices! For pricing options visit:
crconversations.com/Conversation-Club/

Join the club by visiting:
crconversations.com/Conversation-Club/

ACKNOWLEDGEMENTS

My boyfriend Henry, who has truly made me believe that I can do anything I put my mind to. He has supported me in every step of this journey, has been my rock, the love of my life, my advocate and the person who encouraged me to become an entrepreneur. My guiding light, Kimberly Alexander. She has been my mentor, my business strategist, best friend and biggest influence. Without her, this program wouldn't exist.

All my collaborative strategists. Jacki Cox, who has been my FIAT (Friend In All Things), walked with me on this journey, and supported me as my creativity coach to make this book a reality. Donna Galassi, who has been my accountability partner, brand strategist and the reason why my online presence matches my offline personality. Hollie Clere, who has encouraged me, loved me and helped to develop my social media strategies to attract the audience of my dreams. To my Virtual Assistant and dear friend, Abbey, who keeps me sane and is constantly there to support me whether I need something for my business or a glass of wine.

My parents, Emily and Rich, who support me no matter what, brought me up to believe in following my heart and how to live a life of authenticity and love unconditionally. My brother Chris, who has always been my hero. As a veteran and firefighter, he has shown me what compassion and sacrifice truly mean. All those that made this book come to fruition—my editor, publisher and graphic designer—without you, this book would still be a dream. To my followers, clients and friends, this is for you. Without your feedback and honesty, this book would not have any reason for being written.

Fortune is in the Failure